BUT *God*...

I'm
His! Carol

Tired
of
Waiting!

CAROL HOPSON

WINEPRESS WP PUBLISHING

Packaged by WinePress Publishing, PO Box 428, Enumclaw, WA 98022. The views expressed or implied in this work do not necessarily reflect those of WinePress Publishing. Ultimate design, content, and editorial accuracy of this work are the responsibilities of the author.

Unless otherwise noted all scriptures are taken from the New American Standard Bible, © 1960, 1963, 1968, 1971, 1972, 1973, 1975, 1977 by The Lockman Foundation. Used by permission.

Verses marked NIV are taken from the Holy Bible, New International Version, Copyright © 1973, 1978, 1984 by the International Bible Society. Used by permission of Zondervan Publishing House. The "NIV" and "New International Version" trademarks are registered in the United States Patent and Trademark Office by International Bible Society.

Verses marked KJV are taken from the King James Version of the Bible.

ISBN 1-57921-290-5
Library of Congress Catalog Card Number: 00-100800

The following are responses from readers of Carol Hopson's first book, ***But God . . .This Wasn't My Plan!***

"Your book helped me more than I can tell you. I was just about to give up and a friend gave me ***But God . . .This Wasn't My Plan!*** It was exactly what I needed to pull me out of the pit and put me back on track with the Lord."

—Sheri

"I just couldn't get a grip on my problem until I read your book. I thought someone else was to blame for my unhappiness. Thank you for showing me that peace only comes when I choose to obey God's Word."

—Francie

"Thank you, thank you for choosing to be obedient to the Lord. I realized that I had been hanging on to my rights and refusing to go with God's plan. After reading your book, I confessed my selfishness and decided to go with God's Plan. Hallelujah, I'm free and at peace! My deepest thanks!"

—Colleen

"I had just moved to California from another state and was in a deep depression. After hearing you speak, I bought your book, and I wept all the way through it. You put my thoughts into words. I was so uplifted by your story, and I loved all the Scripture you gave to help me be obedient."

—Pam

"This is one of those books I'll pick up and read again and again, and it will continue to speak to me."

—Christie

"No words can express what a lifesaver your book was! I picked it up at the Christian bookstore and wept all the way through. God has cleansed my heart and given me the desire to follow His plan, whatever it may be."

—Brenda

"My wife shared your book with me after she read it. She thought it would help with a situation we were going through, and I just want to tell you how much it helped me. The Scriptures you used were just what we needed to get our attitudes right and change our focus to pleasing God rather than ourselves."

—Paul

"Your book inspired me beyond words. I've shared it with my mom, my sister-in-law, and several friends. They all loved it. Thanks for sharing your story and being so transparent."

—Linda

"I couldn't believe I was reading your story because it seemed just like a story I could have written, except I didn't choose obedience until I read your book. Thank you for showing me the way back to fellowship with the Lord. I'll be forever grateful."

—Nancy

This book is dedicated
to
my loving parents,

Dr. Ralph and Dorothy Kraft,

for
bringing me up in
the nurture and admonition
of the Lord,

for your
constant love and encouragement,
your
godly example in all things,
your
fruitful ministry in the Lord's work,
and
your walk, which always
matched your talk.

I love you!

CONTENTS

INTRODUCTION

We have a full-price offer on your house!" the voice on the line said. How could this be? We had just met with the Realtor to list it and then left to visit our family for Easter. We were eleven months into asking God for direction and a job for my husband. We needed to sell the house, but thought it would take several months and, by then, we'd surely know where we were going. But, no! God had other plans; plans to show His power in other ways. So, He had the first person who walked in the door buy our home.

I loved our home. When we had moved to the Pacific Northwest almost three years earlier, it was out of obedience to the Lord. Previously, we had lived in Solvang, California, near our children, grand-children, and parents. My husband and I had co-founded a Christian School there and had Bible studies and ministries, a growing church, and a newly remodeled home. We were settled! My husband had even built a playhouse for the grand-children in our backyard, but God called us to a new minis-try in Seattle. After many prayers and tears, we gave up our plans and went with His. Now, after three short years, our time here was over suddenly and without warning. In my first book, "But God, This Wasn't My Plan!" I shared about that experience and all the pain and healing that took place while waiting for God to show us the next step.

Now, eleven months later, we've just had a wonderful offer on our home, but we don't know where we are going or what my husband's next job will be. These are truly in-credible days. Some are good, feeling so blessed and com-forted by the Lord; some are not so good, and we feel alone and uncertain.

What do you do while waiting? Some of you may be wait-ing for a wayward child or spouse to return to the Lord. Maybe you're waiting for physical or emotional healing, or possibly, like me, your future is unknown, and you can't figure out what your next step should be. In all of these situations there are certain principles I've learned to help me through the waiting process.

Being far away from family with no job, no income, and no direction from the Lord, was definitely a difficult time to wait patiently! But I knew I needed to put God and His Word to the ultimate test. Were the verses I had memorized years ago really reliable? *Trust in the Lord with all your heart and lean not unto your own understanding. In all your ways acknowledge Him and He will direct your paths (Prov. 3:5,6). The Lord is my Shepherd, I shall not want (Psalm 23:1).*

In the early weeks and months of waiting for employment, my hopes and my trust were high. But choosing to continually trust God when nothing was in sight, money was scarce, and the unknown future loomed ahead of me like a black tunnel became more of a challenge than I ever thought possible. It was during the later months of waiting that I began to journal the lessons I was learning. I pray that God will use what He has taught me through His precious Word to encourage you to be steadfast and immovable in your faith during your waiting process.

LESSONS LEARNED
WHILE WAITING

CHAPTER 1

GOD DOESN'T ALWAYS ANSWER ON OUR TIME SCHEDULE

When my husband's job as Superintendent of a Christian School system ended abruptly in June, my time schedule said that surely another opportunity would come by July or August. He had been so faithful to the Lord in his thirty-three years of Christian ministry and was a man of real faith and integrity. Surely God would honor him by giving him another job—even miraculously—at that late date, to be a testimony of His faithfulness to His servant.

In my time schedule, because we had faithfully served the Lord and been above reproach in our actions and reactions to difficult circumstances, we would not have to do without work for very long and use up what little savings we had. After all, we were in the latter years of our ministry and the need for retirement funds was quickly approaching. I also felt that we wouldn't need to worry about the future or sacrifice our pride any further. We had already been through an extremely difficult, untimely situation and had remained faithful to the Lord and the ministry He put us in. Now it was time for God to show Himself on our behalf so He could be glorified through His children. At least, that's what made sense to me. But another day, another week, another month passed with no job and no answer from the Lord. Why didn't God and I have the same time schedule?

As a young child, I used to practice the piano for one hour every day. It didn't sound very pretty most of the time. I can still remember my mother calling from the kitchen, "Carol, that's a B flat!" as I missed it again and again, making a very unpleasant sound. For months I had to practice scales and fingering exercises, which were not fun and didn't make the wonderful music I heard adults play in church. I used to ask if I could play hymn arrangements or classical pieces because I so wanted to make beautiful music. These scales and exercises were so tiring and boring to the ear. My mother and my teacher always reminded me that the right training was so important in reaching the right goal, and I, as a child, couldn't understand or decide how long the process would be. I needed to trust my teacher to take me through the steps needed to make me a musician.

As I look back, I realize that as a child I could see only the drudgery of the day-to-day practice, but my teacher saw the music that was ahead. She kept encouraging me to be faithful to practice one day at a time and assured me that someday I would reap the rewards. Some days, as I listened to a magnificent pianist bringing such joy to so many, I would be inspired to practice for weeks. Other times, I would think, *I'll never be any good*, and want to quit. The key was to trust my teacher and keep the goal in focus—the beautiful music I could one day play. From my childish perspective, I so often wanted to quit. I am so thankful that wasn't allowed.

It became clear to me that I was still God's child, trying to say when the practice was enough and the song should be complete. Just because I was many years older now didn't mean that I still didn't have a lot to learn. I needed to trust my teacher and keep practicing, but what could I practice?

Trust in the Lord and do good; dwell in the land and cultivate faithfulness. Delight yourself in the Lord and He will give you the desires of your heart. Commit your way to the Lord, trust also in Him, and He will do it. Rest in the Lord and wait patiently for Him; do not fret because of him who prospers in his way, because of the man who carries out wicked schemes. Cease from anger, and forsake wrath; do not fret, it leads only to evildoing. (Ps. 37:3–8)

Overwhelming? Yes! There's so much in just this one passage I can practice, but the first thing God was asking of me, while waiting, was to *trust in the Lord and do good*. That meant daily working on my attitude (trust) and my actions (do). The *trusting* and *doing* go hand-in-hand if I am going to be able to cultivate faithfulness during the waiting process. *I must trust Him to take care of us and our future, and I must do what honors Him on a daily basis.* That meant keeping my thoughts pure, my motives right, and thinking on His truths rather than the bleakness of my circumstances (see Ps. 51:10; Phil. 4:8–9). In other words, when worry would confront me, as it usually did when I went to bed each night, I needed to take each thought *captive to the obedience of Christ* (II Cor. 10:5). Recognizing that worry was a sin, I had to capture it

15

and confess it so that it wouldn't take root in my mind and overtake the fruitful garden God was endeavoring to plant in my life.

I recall going on vacation for over two weeks one summer. I left our garden in the hands of a watering system my husband had hooked up to make sure it would be well-watered in the July heat. When we returned, we couldn't even see the garden for the weeds. They had flourished beyond belief and had completely hidden the tomatoes, lettuce, cucumbers, zucchini, and other produce. It was a huge job to rid our beautiful garden of all those ugly weeds; but it was absolutely necessary if we wanted a productive garden.

Weeds

Weeds, weeds,
always in my garden
choking out the beauty of each row.

Weeds, weeds,
every day some new ones
always seems that they so quickly grow.

Weeds, weeds
creeping into my life
choking out the beauty of His love.

Weeds, weeds,
need to be uprooted,
seeking God to cleanse me from above.

Weeds, weeds,
never need to be there
if my garden's daily in His care!

—*Carol Hopson*

Those ugly weeds of worry, doubt, fear, or frustration would sprout up at the most unexpected times and seem to overtake the joy the Lord had planted in my heart just hours before. That's why daily weed-pulling became a very important routine for me. Even one day left untended could allow deep roots of doubt to settle in, and I'd wonder where my joy had gone.

Dear Father, please forgive me for allowing thoughts that dishonor You to take root today. Please cleanse the garden of my mind and plant your beauty in it. Allow others to see your fragrance in me by observing my countenance and my contentment today so that You will be glorified through your servant in the garden of my life. Amen.

Another reason God might have had a different time schedule was to glorify Himself in a different way than I thought best. We can't always choose our form of service, and He wanted others to observe us going through the fire. He wanted me to speak on faith, joy, perseverance, and holiness while in the midst of a drought. God allowed me a whole year of sharing His sufficiency in the midst of real pain and uncertainty. Countless women shared how much it ministered to them that I was in the middle of the storm, but at peace. Let me assure you that peace was a moment-by-moment choice I had to make, and not an automatic song. But as I chose to be obedient, God was teaching me so much more about the music He intended for my life. I learned that faith is not having things all figured out and then asking God to come along and bless them. And it's certainly not expecting God to work a certain way and then falling into discouragement when it doesn't happen. *Faith is trusting God, period!* **It is trusting His timing and the situations He allows to work for my good, because I trust His love for me and believe His word.**

And we know that God causes all things to work together for good to those who love God, to those who are called according to His purpose. (Rom. 8:28)

CHAPTER 2

LISTENING TO FRIENDS CAN CAUSE DISILLUSIONMENT

Each time I spoke at a retreat or conference, some well-meaning Christian would approach me afterwards and share, "Oh, my husband was laid off for three months, but now he has a better job than ever, with more money than he's ever made, and we are so happy." I knew that this was meant to encourage me, but it seemed to have the opposite effect. Was a better job and more money what brought happiness and contentment? Was I to assume that the loss we experienced would automatically bring us to great things, humanly speaking? I seldom, if ever, heard one of these saints say, "It was a very difficult time for us, but oh, how we grew in our understanding of

God's grace and sufficiency." Beyond that, the purpose of sharing with me seemed to be to tell me to just wait and endure and something good would finally happen. If the heartache of waiting was always followed by material abundance, as I was so often led to believe, we'd all be clamoring for more trials.

Each time a dear sister or brother in the Lord used this type of "encouragement," it brought me to my knees and back to God's word for real strengthening and revival. God's word does promise to give me the desires of my heart and direct my paths, but those desires need to be in line with my Heavenly Father's will, not with what friends think I should or should not have. The God who made me is the only one who can strengthen me.

> My soul weeps because of grief; strengthen me according to Thy word. Remove the false way from me and graciously grant me Thy law. I have chosen the faithful way; I have placed Thine ordinances before me. I cleave to Thy testimonies O Lord, do not put me to shame! I shall run the way of Thy commandments, for Thou wilt enlarge my heart. (Ps. 119:28–32)

To learn while waiting, my choice needed to be to *run the way of God's words* and constantly *remove the false way* that was brought before me. If I choose to vigorously follow God's truths, He will *enlarge my heart*. This enlarging speaks of the wisdom He will give to help me through any situation. If I truly choose the *faithful way*, I will, as I read in this passage, place God's *ordinances before me*. I have been known to place scripture verses all around my home and office. While working as a school secretary and assistant to my husband, I was challenged daily to, *Let no unwholesome words proceed from my mouth but only such a word as is good for edification according to the need of the moment, that it may give grace to those who hear it* (Eph. 4:29). I kept that verse taped to my phone for over ten years. Though I knew it from memory, there were days when I needed to focus on it visually, keeping it before my eyes, and deciding to obey it.

One day, after teaching the Mother's Bible study and returning to my office, a very frustrated parent came in and shouted, "You're not God, you know!" As I waited in silence for what was to follow, I was treated to a mouthful of rhetoric against what God's word says about submission, forgiveness, and humility. It wasn't outwardly aimed at God. It was aimed at me, the teacher. How dare I tell her she needed to submit to her husband and be an example to her children. How dare I teach that there was a Biblical pattern for the home, and it wasn't that the wife should be the head. As she announced that she was smarter than her husband and I was a fool if I let my husband be the head of our home, I looked down at the reminder on my phone and asked God to calm my heart and give grace to the hearer.

Let me assure you that I don't like being attacked, and I desperately wanted to defend myself, but the Lord shut my mouth—miraculously! After a moment of silence, she spouted, "Well, what do you have to say for yourself?" I glanced at my desk again, where I had a small reminder that read, *The Love of Christ constrains me*. I responded with, "Jesus in me, loves you." Well, that definitely was not what she expected. As she stood and stared at me, completely dumbfounded, I could see that God's grace had started to penetrate her hardened heart. She walked away that day and I bowed my head and prayed.

Through the next months and years she came to me to help her give her life to the Lord, and she continually asked for counsel as to what a Christian home should be like. She learned to ask God for help with her quick temper and her pride, and God gave us a wonderful, lasting relationship. I believe that having God's written words before me that day made a difference for eternity in one woman's life.

He Leadeth Me

He leadeth me
　　through pathways straight
　　when detours beckon at my gate.

He leadeth me
　　to sing His praise
　　through clouded skies and rainy days.

He leadeth me
　　to victory
　　when life seems such a mystery.

He leadeth me
　　to life complete
　　when others say "there's no such feat."

He leadeth me
　　to turn to Him
　　when times are tough and hope grows dim.

He leadeth me
　　on every side
　　if I will in His Word abide.

—*Carol Hopson*

So, what *ordinances* or scriptures should we set before us while waiting? We never know when we'll have the opportunity to make a difference in someone's life.

Words for waiting!

I pray that out of His glorious riches He may strengthen you with power through His Spirit in your inner being, so that Christ may dwell in your hearts through faith. And I pray that you, being rooted and established in love, may have power, together with all the saints, to grasp how wide and long and high and deep is the love of Christ, and to know this love that surpasses knowledge, that you may be filled to the measure of all the fullness of God. (Eph. 3:16–19, NIV)

This "strengthening with power" refers to a special degree of grace that God gives and the spiritual ability to resist the temptation to be discouraged or give up. His strength in our inner being enables us to persevere while waiting, to persevere when misunderstood, and to persevere in bearing fruit during the times of drought.

These words of wisdom go on to say that we should pray that we would be "rooted and established in love." This means to be steadfastly fixed on His love for me and my complete love for Him, in any situation, at all times. If I trust how much He loves me, because He gave His most precious possession, His beloved Son, I can respond with unconditional love and trust Him to see me through this waiting time. There were many days in our year of waiting for a job that I truly experienced this kind of trust, but there were others when my trust was conditioned on whether or not I could see something encouraging ahead. That is not trust! That is not listening to God's Words! Remember the promise, *The steadfast of mind, Thou wilt keep in perfect peace, because he trusts in*

Thee (Isa. 26:3). **When I was not at peace, it was always because my mind was no longer steadfast on the love of God and His Word.**

If you are struggling right now because you've been waiting for God to heal a relationship, bring a loved one to the Lord, restore a wayward child, or give you a healthy body, check your thoughts. What are you dwelling on? Psalm 18 reminds us that, *The Lord is near to the brokenhearted, and saves those who are crushed in spirit. Many are the afflictions of the righteous; but the Lord delivers him out of them all.* Sometimes He delivers us from the situation; but most of the time, he delivers me from discouragement in the situation and restores the joy of my salvation (Ps. 51:12).

CHAPTER 3

I Can't Just Focus on Getting Out of My Circumstances!

Why not? I can hear you asking that question right now, and I'm quick to admit that I tried it many times. But the Bible doesn't teach that, so we have to look at what God intends for us to focus on while waiting.

When my husband battled back problems and was in and out of treatment and hospitals for several years, I kept thinking, "When this is all over and my husband is well, I'll be able to be truly content and happy again." I fell into the same snare when I was terribly ill and couldn't eat anything for months. I would wake up and think, "I'll be so happy when I can eat again, but in the meantime I've just got to survive." Do we see any escape clauses in Scripture?

Therefore, since we have so great a cloud of witnesses surrounding us, let us also lay aside every encumbrance, and the sin which so easily entangles us and let us run with endurance the race that is set before us, fixing our eyes on Jesus, the author and perfecter of faith who for the joy set before Him endured the cross, despising the shame and has sat down at the right hand of the throne of God. For consider Him who has endured such hostility by sinners against Himself so that you may not grow weary and lose heart. (Heb. 12:1–3)

Lay Aside Every Encumbrance

What is an encumbrance? It is anything that pulls you down, or hinders you from freedom of action, or freedom to serve and obey God. It is like a dead weight that pulls us down to be consumed with worry over temporal things, rather than being lifted upward toward eternal values. So what encumbers us when we're waiting—our unresolved hopes and dreams, fear of the unknown, fear that God might ask too much of us, and worry that we won't like His plan? These are all encumbrances that we must lay aside and get rid of.

Not only are we to get rid of the weights, but we are to confess the sin that *so easily entangles us.* I come from a family that loves to fish! My dad and older twin brothers would often let me tag along when we were camping. I learned at an early age to bait my hook, cast the line into the stream, and then wait for that sudden tug that makes a fisherman's heart leap. Sometimes, a beautiful rainbow trout was on the other end, but other times the sudden tug was a tangle. My line was caught in the rocks or branches below the water line. It couldn't be seen from my point of view, but it certainly changed my ability to catch fish. Nothing could be accomplished until I was untangled and put fresh bait on the hook. My patient father would wade into the ice cold stream and untangle my line so I could begin the process again, with fresh bait and renewed hope.

What a lesson this was for me! My entanglements usually came below the water, unseen at first, like the wrong thoughts that are below the surface and go unnoticed for a while. Worry sets in, or resentment because of an unjust situation, or maybe discouragement due to waiting, and the hook is caught. This is the entanglement of sin. Nothing good can happen; no fruit can come from my branches, until I'm disentangled by confessing my sin, and I put new bait on the hook by reviving my soul through fellowship with the Lord and meditating on His word. Then my countenance will change, my purpose will again become clear, and I once again will be attractive to those who seek Christ (Col. 1:10–12).

Run the race with endurance

I noticed that endurance is mentioned three times in the first eight verses of the Hebrews twelve passage, so we need to know what it means to run with endurance. To carry on despite hardship, to bear with tolerance, to continually persevere, or to suffer patiently without yielding to temptation, all could describe how we are to run the race of life. Each of us has a specific race we are to run, unlike any other's. For me, discouragement came when I looked at other people's circumstances and saw that they weren't going through the difficult things God was allowing me to go through. My human heart would ask, "Why is God allowing me to go through such pain when I'm trying to serve Him so faithfully?" Each time I had to go back to God's Word and see that my race was planned so that I could glorify God and bear fruit in the midst of **my** situation. This would touch lives that couldn't be reached any other way.

27

It seemed that God chose to reveal much of the fruit only after our year of drought. My husband and I received many notes and e-mails after we moved into our new ministry, but one especially thrilled me.

Knowing the situation and pain you were going through, I was watching to see if bitterness or anger would rear its head in your lives. I want to tell you that I never saw any of it. I only saw God's servants continuing to be faithful in trusting God with their deepest needs. I want to tell you that it has strengthened my faith more than you will ever know. If God can do that for you, I know He will do it for me if I let Him.

This aspect of running with endurance became so evident to me as I spoke at conferences and retreats during our "waiting time"—which was the most fruitful ministry God has blessed me with thus far. God definitely showed me that His plan was to use the difficult waiting time to teach me humility, patience, and His sufficiency, so that I could model it for others and give them hope. But He also knew that I needed to know the depth of their pain and the difficult choice of trusting even in the darkest night.

The Darkest Night

I thought that I would never doubt
the love God had for me.
I've known Him for so many years
and served Him faithfully.

I often spoke to many hearts
about God's loving care;
and how they shouldn't worry so,
that He'd be just and fair.

I've even shared my own strong faith
through storms that shook my life.
And told how only trusting God
would keep from doubt and strife.

But God, with love, saw deep inside
this human heart so frail.
And though I felt unshakable
He knew I needed to fail.

To understand how others feel
when all their hope is gone.
To feel their pain and know their hurt
and the darkness before dawn.

And so He had me wait until
my heart could bear no more,
as each job option came and went,
with nothing new in store.

The circumstances, hopeless seemed,
and darker grew the night.
But God taught me with each new day
to walk by faith, not sight.

To claim each promise in His word
and clutch them to my breast.
For only when I ceased to doubt
did my heart truly rest.

—*Carol Hopson*

And without faith it is impossible to please God . . .
(Hebrews 12:6)

Fixing Our Eyes on Jesus

Jesus was and is our example of how to run the race set before us. He trusted His Father in life and death, and in humiliation and pain. He was the finisher of grace by His death on the cross because His eyes were fixed on His Father's will at any cost.

When my husband and I felt God leading us to start a Christian School in the Santa Ynez Valley, one of the many details was choosing a mascot for the school. After much prayer, we chose the eagle because of the scriptures that relate to the eagle, and the desire for the students to learn from the unique characteristics of the eagle. An eagle is rarely sick because of carefully choosing his diet; but when he does become ill, he will choose a high cliff or butte and lie with his wings spread out, facing the sun. He will then focus his eyes on the sun until the warmth of the sun heals his body and he is ready to soar again. What a great picture this gives us of our own need to fix our eyes on the "Son" for healing and reviving.

David knew the absolute importance of being revived by focusing on God's word:

> Great are Thy mercies, O Lord; revive me according to Thine ordinances. Many are my persecutors and my adversaries, yet I do not turn aside from Thy testimonies. I behold the treacherous and loathe them, because they do not keep Thy word. Consider how I love Thy precepts; revive me, O Lord, according to Thy lovingkindness. The sum of Thy word is truth, and every one of Thy righteous ordinances is everlasting. (Ps. 119:156–160)

The 119th Psalm has meant a great deal to believers down through the years. William Wilberforce, the statesman who was converted in the Wesleyan movement, wrote in his diary,

"Walked from Hyde Park corner, repeating the 119th Psalm in great comfort." Can you imagine the comfort we would receive if we could recite all one hundred and seventy- six verses of this precious portion of God's word? All but two verses praise the word of God and proclaim its benefits to us. So, by keeping our eyes fixed on Jesus as our example, and on the living Word of God, we will be able to wait with endurance, patience and purpose.

For the Joy Set before Him

Jesus endured what the Father had planned because of the joy set before Him. What then was His joy? It was the greater cause of redemption, peace between God and man, and the joy of total obedience to His Father (Phil. 2:5–11).

This seems so obvious to us when we look at the plan of salvation, but what is the joy set before us? I'd like to suggest four things that we can focus on as our joy during the long waiting periods in our lives.

1. We have the joy of magnifying Christ to others.

Paul shows us his focus in Philippians 1:20: *According to my earnest expectation and my hope, that in nothing I should be ashamed, but that with all boldness, Christ shall be magnified in my body, whether it be by life or by death* (KJV). To magnify is to enlarge, clarify, or make something easier to see. Our joy, while waiting, should be to enlarge and clarify the presence and power of the Lord in our lives. Unfortunately, we all fall short of this at times and distort the truth of God's lovingkindness and sovereignty. We rely on our emotions and dwell on our situation rather than on the truths of God's words. That's why focusing on the Son must be our stability if we are to "magnify" Christ to those around us.

2. We have the joy of God's daily guidance in our lives.

For I am confident of this very thing, that He who began a good work in you will perfect it until the day of Christ Jesus. (Phil. 1:6)

The steps of a man are established by the Lord; and He delights in his way. When he falls, he shall not be hurled headlong; because the Lord is the One who holds his hand. (Ps. 37:23,24)

Trust in the Lord with all your heart and do not lean on your own understanding. In all your ways acknowledge Him and He will make your paths straight. (Prov. 3:5,6)

When we really grasp the fact that God wants to show us how to live each day, we begin to open our eyes to His perspective, rather than ours. Recently, while meeting a friend for lunch at a newly designed shopping center in a quaint little village, I looked in all the shop windows to see how they were decorated and whether there were signs of sales or bargains. I glanced quickly at what stores were available and which ones might be interesting and affordable. It took me by surprise when my friend voiced her awe at the architecture of the buildings and walkways. She pointed out the uniqueness of each arbor, textured wall, and stone or brick walkway. She absolutely delighted in the beauty of it and the quality of the workmanship. I could have been there all day and never noticed any of the buildings had it not been for her perspective on our surroundings. Why did she and I see such different things in the very same place? *Because we were looking for different things.* My agenda in a shopping center is to look for bargains. Hers was to look at the architecture and learn from it since she was involved in that business.

This experience revealed to me the importance of seeking God's perspective for my daily journey. I'm missing so much of the joy, and probably much of His guidance, when I just see it through my own eyes and my own agenda. So, I learned to begin each day with a prayer that would open my eyes to what He wanted me to see for that particular day.

Dear God, thank you for today. Thank you that You are with me to see me through all my doubts and fears. Please open my eyes to see what you want me to see today and learn what you have for me. I want to know Your will. I want to be obedient and glorify You in whatever You bring into, or take out of, my life today because I love You more than anything or anyone else. Please help me to be faithful, just for today. Amen.

3. We have the joy of future reward.

Blessed is a man who perseveres under trial; for once he has been approved, he will receive the crown of life, which the Lord has promised to those who love Him. (James 1:12)

Beloved, do not be surprised at the fiery ordeal among you, which comes upon you for your testing, as though some strange thing were happening to you; but to the degree that you share the sufferings of Christ, keep on rejoicing; so that also at the revelation of His glory, you may rejoice with exultation. (I Peter 4:12,13)

Do you remember the joy of finding that perfect gift for someone you love? Maybe it was your mate, or your teenager, or your mother, who has always been there for you. When I think of how much thought I put into each Christmas and birthday gift for my family members, I am reminded that God has told me what He wants as a gift from me. While speaking at a retreat, someone handed me the following:

The Gift

I heard today
Of a decrepit native woman
Who walked mile after mile
Under blistering sun
To bring a small gift of embroidery
To the missionary she deeply loved.
Hour after hour she trudged
Over rough, rugged roads
Clutching tightly her small gift.
Her weary body sagged
Her vision blurred
Her bare feet bled from the jagged rocks.

Grateful but overwhelmed
The missionary wept.
The trembling old woman spoke softly:
"Please understand.
The walk is part of the gift."

My Lord
My commitment to You is for life.
I give myself to You unreservedly
To do with me as You please.
But may I not forget
That the tears, the fears
The strain, and the pain
The sunless days
The star-less nights
Are all a part of the whole.

In my total commitment
I give full consent;
The walk is part of the gift.

—*Ruth Harms Calkin*

Do we truly love the Lord enough to make the waiting part of the gift? This is what He desires of us. Can you take your own struggle, loved one, or circumstance, and place them in a beautiful box marked "To Jesus, with love." Then picture yourself placing it at Jesus feet, as a love gift for giving His life for you. Do you love Him that much?

4. We have the joy of peace stemming from our obedience.

I remember the thrill and anticipation of helping my daughter plan her wedding. What an exciting time of life. I had looked forward to the day she would marry a wonderful Christian man since she was born, and now it was becoming a reality. The only problem was that she and I had different ideas of what she would wear, what the decorations would be, what the cake would be like and so on. As we spent time together shopping, I began to feel hurt and upset that she didn't always like the same things I did and plan her wedding accordingly. I know how selfish this sounds. That's because it was! I wanted what I liked, period. Fortunately, the Holy Spirit was prodding me and convicting me that my will and pride were getting in the way of something truly wonderful. I had to confess to her and to the Lord my wrong attitude and give up my plans. An immediate relief flooded me, and I was free to share in the real joy of planning "her" wedding—not mine! The joy that came out of that obedience made the whole wedding experience absolutely wonderful. Everything she chose was just right, but I couldn't see it until I listened to the Holy Spirit and gave up my pride.

When we're waiting for God's answers, we have an incredible opportunity to learn about the joy of obedience. **This joy will never come from outward conformity, but only from inward conviction and a heart that is ready to obey at all costs.**

CHAPTER 4

WAITING REQUIRES ABSOLUTE TRUST

S uppose for a moment, that you took a letter to the mailbox and put it in the slot, but you held on to the very tip of the envelope. Then you waited and waited, wondering why you never received an answer to your letter. You see, you almost mailed it, didn't you? Does that work? Of course not, and yet that is how we often bring our concerns to the Lord. We take them to His throne in prayer, and then, when we leave, we hang onto them with worry or fear and expect Him to answer.

> *But if any of you lacks wisdom, let him ask of God, who gives to all men generously and without reproach, and it will be given to him. But let*

*him ask in faith without any doubting, for the one who doubts
is like the surf of the sea driven and tossed by the wind. For let
not that man expect that he will receive anything from the Lord.
(James 1:5–7)*

God has made it so clear to us, yet we get frustrated with
waiting and wonder why we're not experiencing peace, or
seeing Him work on our behalf. In the book of Numbers we
find a great example of this. In chapter 13, verse 2, the Lord
spoke to Moses saying, *Send out for yourself men so that they
may spy out the land of Canaan, which I am going to give to the
sons of Israel.* Do you see that promise from Almighty God?
With the instruction is the truth that God is going to give
them the land of Canaan. We read on to find that upon their
return, they gave the following report:

*We went in to the land where you sent us; and it certainly does
flow with milk and honey, and this is its fruit. Nevertheless,
the people who live in the land are strong, and the cities are
fortified and very large; and moreover, we saw the descendants of Anak there. (v. 27–28) We are not able to go up
against the people, for they are too strong for us. So they gave
out to the sons of Israel a bad report of the land which they had
spied out. (v. 31–32)*

Notice how this report affected the people.

*Then all the congregation lifted up their voices and cried, and
the people wept that night. And all the sons of Israel grumbled
against Moses and Aaron; and the whole congregation said to
them, "Would that we had died in the land of Egypt! Or would
that we had died in this wilderness! And why is the Lord bringing us into this land, to fall by the sword? Our wives and our
little ones will become plunder; would it not be better for us to
return to Egypt?" (14:1–3)*

First of all, we see the major mistake that the spies made. **They looked at the circumstances rather than the promise of God, and it resulted in great fear.** When fear comes on the scene, by our own choice, it defeats us because it is really based on a lack of trust. That unbelief then changes our countenance, our perspective, our hope, and eventually, our desires. Rather than desiring to read God's precious word and develop a closer relationship with Him through prayer, we pull away. We stop practicing the very things that make the waiting process fruitful and fall into a deeper pit of despair. It all begins with a choice to doubt God's Words.

We also note in this story that while God is trusting us with a waiting period, whether long or short, there is a *congregation*, a group of people, that we are affecting either negatively or positively for the Lord. We see in this passage that after hearing the report, they cried, wept, grumbled, and doubted the Lord. Furthermore, they didn't even want the great things God had in store for them. They wanted to go back to Egypt. When I read that, I was amazed at their lack of faith and their utter despair, despite God's words promising to give them the land. Then I looked at my own life and my struggles in waiting, and I remembered how human and frail I am, and how easy it is to get caught up in the hopelessness of the daily struggle. Through several major waiting rooms in my life, God has deeply rooted in me the importance of complete, unwavering trust—without knowing why I have to wait or when it will end.

Think of how different this story would be if all the spies had believed God and therefore, had inspired the Israelites to trust God and watch Him keep His word. Instead, the Lord responds with:

How long will this people spurn Me. And how long will they not believe in Me, despite all the signs which I have performed in their midst? (14:12)

Surely all the men who have seen My glory and My signs, which I performed in Egypt and in the wilderness, yet have put Me to the test these ten times and have not listened to My voice, shall by no means see the land which I swore to their fathers, nor shall any of those who spurned Me see it. (14:22–23)

They missed the "promised land" because of unbelief. What might you be missing in your situation because of unbelief? What could be your "promised land"? There could be family members watching your reactions to see if God truly does "supply all our needs" during the tough times. Can you think of anything greater than having someone you love and have prayed for come to the Lord because of your faithfulness in the trenches? There could be a "promised land" on the other side of our situation, but we're too discouraged to move on or be open to what God might do.

When my husband and I were waiting for God to show us what He wanted us to do after thirty-three years in the Christian School ministry, there were definitely days when we thought of giving up and taking a job that wasn't where our hearts were. When fear and discouragement were allowed to grow in our minds, our priorities would change and we would think of settling for anything, rather than God's best. But as we prayed, we knew that God had still given us a desire to minister in Christian Education. We had to trust that He would provide a Canaan for us in His time. After eleven long months, God took us to a wonderful place in a tremendous Christian School where He has poured out His blessings upon us. It was so important for us to keep our hearts and minds open and expect God to work, or we would have missed this "promised land".

God's words to Caleb were so different from those to the Israelites. *But my servant Caleb, because he has had a different spirit and has followed Me fully, I will bring into the land which he*

entered, and his descendants shall take possession of it (14:24).
If we expect God to bless us, His words are very clear. We
must have a *different spirit* than the world's when in a difficult
situation, and we must *fully follow Him*.

Picture, for a moment, you and a travel guide on a long
walk through a wooded forest. As you begin, the guide warns
you to follow him closely, as there are many places to get lost
or get off the path. At first you follow closely, watching his
feet continually, especially through the tangles of the forest.
But then you begin to get more comfortable. You look around
more and take your eyes off the guide. You slow down in your
fervor. Before long you've become lost because you didn't
"fully follow" the guide. There is no such thing as *sort of* following! We either follow fully, or we don't follow Him at all.

Following the Leader

The game of life is at its best
a game of choices made,
to choose this job, select that road,
as other options fade.

Each choice brings many twists and turns
along the path of life
And how we handle all that comes
brings joy or endless strife.

So what determines how we live
and which way we should go?
Are we headed for destruction,
Is there something we should know?

Again, we must remember that
God's Word is all we need.

And as we choose obedience
we're following His lead.

So following our Leader strong
while waiting, helps us stand.
We realize we're not alone
but walking hand in hand.

—*Carol Hopson*

CHAPTER 5

THE LONELINESS OF WAITING HAS A PURPOSE

One of the most difficult emotions we experience while waiting is loneliness. It can be overwhelming because we feel no one is going through what we are, and no one really understands or cares about us. This is especially true for a single parent who is carrying the financial and emotional responsibilities for the home. He or she often feels so alone and can't see any purpose in it, only pain.

The eagle gives us some insight into the purpose of loneliness. After a fledgling eagle leaves the nest, he will not mate for at least three years. He will use this time to live alone, become a skilled hunter, fly at higher altitudes than any other bird, and observe the earth. It is during this time that he studies the currents of the wind and masters them so that in a storm, he can use the currents of the storm to help lift him above it. Other creatures are fearful and restless in a storm, but the eagle waits patiently, studying the different currents he has learned from his lonely years. Then he masters the wind and puts it under his feet. The storm still rages, but he rises above it and gains a new perspective. During the three years of isolation, he is not sidetracked to go with other birds or to build a nest. He is determined to be prepared for what lies ahead.

Why do we think there's something wrong with loneliness? Many of God's faithful servants had lonely times that equipped them for service. When Elijah was fleeing from Jezebel we read, *And he was afraid and arose and ran for his life and came to Beersheba, which belongs to Judah and left his servant there. But he himself went a day's journey into the wilderness, and came and sat down under a juniper tree; and he requested for himself that he might die, and said, "It is enough; now, O Lord, take my life, for I am not better than my father." And he lay down and slept under a juniper tree; and behold, there was an angel touching him, and he said to him, "Arise, eat." Then he looked and behold, there was at his head a bread cake baked on hot stones, and a jar of water. So he ate and drank and lay down again (I Kings 19:3–6).* After this, we discover that Elijah went in the strength of that food for forty days and nights to Mount Horeb, the mountain of God. There God spoke to him and gave him directions for the future. Through the loneliness, Elijah discovered anew the provision, strength, and personal involvement of the Lord in his life.

I would be disobedient to God's word if I didn't share, at this point, about how much I grew in my understanding of God's faithfulness during each waiting period of my life. I am reminded in Psalm 34 that, *I will bless the Lord at all times; His praise shall continually be in my mouth. My soul shall make its* boast in the Lord; the humble shall hear it and rejoice (Psalm 34:1–2). My only boasting can and will be that the Lord was all I needed to see me through.

All I Need

Wouldn't it be wonderful if I could plant the seed,
That gave wings to a famous song, but You are all I need.

Wouldn't it be wonderful if I could write a creed
That established peace for everyone, but You are all I need.

Wouldn't it be wonderful if I someone could lead
To change his ways and mend his life, but You are all I need.

Wouldn't it be wonderful if one could somewhere read
A book that I had authored, but You are all I need.

Wouldn't it be wonderful if all these things came true.
But my future plans are in Your hands, 'cause all I need is You.

—Carol Hopson
September 1986

Jeremiah, Nehemiah, Job, Paul, David, and even our Lord Jesus, had lonely times. But they were not without a purpose. Paul used his lonely times to write the scriptures, to encourage others, to witness to the prison guards. What incredible, lasting fruit he bore in his loneliness. David says, *It is good for me that I was afflicted, that I may learn Thy statutes. The law of Thy mouth is better to me than thousands of gold and silver pieces* (Ps. 119:71–72).

When my husband and I were led by God to start a Christian School in Solvang, California, we became very aware of the loneliness of waiting. We opened our school in a small church which, realistically, only had room for fifty students. It was always our intent to move and expand the ministry in the first few years. But as our student body tripled, we still had no place to move. For thirteen years we tried to find new property for our school. For thirteen years our hopes would rise as we researched seventeen different locations and possibilities for a school site. Each time we wondered if this was God's plan. Then our hopes would fall when it fell through again. At one point we purchased a large piece of property where we were going to build a new school. After three years of entanglements with the Board of Supervisors and the Planning Commission, we were to have our final approval hearing. We had spent thousands and thousands of dollars and innumerable hours making sure all issues were resolved and all conditions were met for approval, but we knew the enemy did not want the school to survive. Many had come to create discord.

As I awaited the hearing, I sat in the large meeting room and wrote down what God was putting on my heart for that day.

Dear Lord, help me to be an empty page, ready for you to write on today. Help me to erase any anxiety, anger, or doubt that would blotch up this page of my life.

Heavenly Father, as I listen to You and not to others, fill this page of my life with your love and understanding. Let peace be the main theme and keep selfish desires from ruining the script, as they sneak in whenever I'm not looking at You.

Today, Lord, many will read this page and get a glimpse of You and Your power to sustain and strengthen Your child. May the writing be clear and true and may my page encourage others to seek You. This is my prayer for today, Father.

Lovingly, Carol

You see, there were hundreds of people there to see if the Christian Academy would finally get its new school. It had been in the papers almost daily over the past couple of years. The city leaders and a few residents didn't want the school built, so they had waged a battle of lies and misinformation. My husband and I and our godly board members felt very alone that day physically, but we were strengthened by God's presence.

The Board of Supervisors voted us down. Suddenly all our years of working, waiting, dreaming, and ministering seemed to be shut down—but God was still in it! He gave us calm, sweet spirits as we left that room with many looking on, and He gave us the strength and encouragement to continue. Six months later I was in the grocery store when a man approached me and said, "You and your husband are the ones who started that Christian School, aren't you?" I responded that we were. He went on, "I had read about the school over the years and wondered what you Christians were really like. The only ones I've known have been hypocrites. But I watched you at that hearing, and you were different. Thank you for living what you preach." Then he walked away.

It would be many more years of waiting before God revealed His perfect plan of a beautiful new school—completely donated to us, on the most prime corner we could ever have hoped for. He was so faithful, and we learned a great deal about waiting and worshipping without worry.

Now, many years later, here I was again in that familiar place of waiting. I didn't want to waste it. How valuable God's word became to me when I felt so alone. I had always thought I really treasured God's word. After all, I had spent the last thirty years studying and teaching it to women's groups and Bible Study groups. I know that I loved it and loved teaching it, but my hunger became so great, and the words were so alive and nutritious, that I couldn't get enough. My appetite became voracious as there was little else to sidetrack me, and my need was great. Can you see the purpose of loneliness? It can bring us to a place of exceptional growth, understanding, and personal fellowship with our Lord.

Thy word is very pure, therefore Thy servant loves it. I am small and despised, yet I do not forget Thy precepts. Thy righteousness is an everlasting righteousness, and Thy law is truth. Trouble and anguish have come upon me; yet Thy commandments are my delight. (Ps. 119:140–143)

Remember how the eagle was preparing for future storms while he was in his three lonely years? We, too, are preparing for what lies ahead. We are being made into something beautiful and extraordinary. Sapphires, agates, diamonds, and precious stones are all jewels, but what exactly is a jewel? It begins as a lump of ordinary, possibly ugly, piece of clay or stone. So where does the beauty come from? Why are some stones so much more beautiful and valuable? It is because they have passed through a process which is called crystallization. During this process, they have gone through exceptional circumstances, immense pressure, and intense heat—maybe even over centuries. It is the extraordinary circumstances that have produced the beauty.

If we desire to be jewels that shine brilliantly for the Lord, we must submit willingly to the intense heat, the loneliness, and the difficult circumstances that He allows, and draw ever closer to Him because of it. He has lessons for life that we can only learn by soaring alone. *Yet those who wait for the Lord will gain new strength; they will mount up with wings like eagles, they will run and not get tired, they will walk and not become weary (Isa. 40:31).*

CHAPTER 6

I MUST LET GO OF THE HURT!

It seems to me that most waiting periods involve being hurt. There is the hurt from an unfaithful or un-loving spouse, the hurt of a rebellious child, the hurt of an alcoholic parent, the hurt of betrayal by a friend, or the hurt of unfulfilled dreams. Each of these contribute to the difficulty of waiting because we're so filled with the pain caused by someone else's actions.

In our case, the pain of being out of a job, suddenly and without warning, was seemingly caused by one person's actions. The temptation for me was to focus on the person who had brought this pain into our lives. That is how Satan wanted to entrap me and keep me from moving on and finding peace in the midst of the circumstance. As long as I focused on the person, I could have no victory, because I was leaving God out of the equation. I was denying God's power and putting it into another human's hands. I was allowing this person to rob me of joy and peace.

So what do we do with the hurt caused by other's choices or unjust situations? Here are some choices that may seem all too familiar.

You Can Nurse the Hurt

A nurse takes care of someone and tends to their needs. If you nurse your hurt, you take care of it, and nurture it, and allow it to rest inside you. You don't want to give it up, because it gives you comfort to talk about it and hang onto the unjustness of it. *And keep a good conscience so that in the thing in which you are slandered, those who revile your good behavior in Christ may be put to shame. For it is better, if God should will it so, that you suffer for doing what is right rather than for doing what is wrong (I Pet. 3:16–17).*

You Can Curse the Hurt

If you curse the hurt, you become an angry, bitter person. Life is so unfair, and you've been singled out to suffer the most. You view everyone and everything through a bitter spirit, and, therefore, can't see how anything good can come out of your pain. *And so, as those who have been chosen of God, holy and beloved, put on a heart of compassion, kindness, humility, gentleness and patience; bearing with one another, and forgiving each other, whoever has a complaint against anyone; just as the Lord forgave you, so also should you (Col. 3:12–13).*

You Can Rehearse the Hurt

This is my personal favorite. I think I have a Master's degree in rehearsing the hurt. I can lie awake at night and go over and over each word that was said, or what I should have done, or the *what ifs* of the situation. I can write long essays in my mind of what I'd like to say to a specific individual to set him or her straight. But all of this has no value—except to keep me from listening to the Holy Spirit's voice. *Finally, brethren, whatever is true, whatever is honorable, whatever is right, whatever is pure, whatever is lovely, whatever is of good repute, if there is any excellence and if anything worthy of praise, let your mind dwell on these things (Phil. 4:8).*

You Can Disperse the Hurt

Because you've been hurt, you will now make sure that everyone around you hurts. Usually, this begins at home with those you love; your whole family suffers because of it. You will also tell others what happened, making sure to hurt reputations and bring others down with you. I wonder what we do with Ephesians 4:29? *Let no unwholesome words proceed from your mouth, but only such a word as is good for edification, according to the need of the moment, that it may give grace to those who hear.*

You Can Immerse the Hurt

This is dangerous because you may look like you're handling the pain just fine, but really, you've just buried it deep inside. You really don't want to deal with it because it's too painful. You hope it will just go away, but it doesn't. The seeds of bitterness are planted because it hasn't been given over to the Lord's keeping. Bitterness can rear its ugly head at any point. *See to it that no one comes short of the grace of God; that no root of bitterness springing up causes trouble, and by it many be defiled (Heb. 12:15).*

As you can see, none of these choices are in keeping with what God's word says. So what are we supposed to do with the hurt?

You Can Reverse the Hurt!

I have to admit that sometimes this is humanly impossible. But, with God's help, *all things are possible*, so we need to know how we can reverse the way we're feeling. I recently read the story of Arthur and Wilda Mathews, the last China Inland Mission members to escape from Communist China in 1953. Their story is one of many disappointments and pain, but they learned the secrets of reversing the hurt.

Arthur and Wilda and their small baby, Lilah, had just arrived at their destination in Hwangyuan, China. They had looked forward to this moment for so long and had spent years preparing for their work. They had definitely been called by God to be missionaries to the Mongols. When they received a personal letter inviting them to help in the work at this mission compound, they knew it was God's answer to their prayers. But things did not go as planned. They arrived to a very cool reception by the Chinese missionaries, and were told the compound home they had been promised was not available. This left them to live in a small kitchen with only a table, two chairs, and shelves for food storage. Their hearts were sick, but they went to the Lord in prayer, willing to live like this to reach the Mongols for the Lord.

The next blow came when they were told that they would not be allowed to do the work they were sent to do, which was to help evangelize the Chinese church. They were told foreigners were looked down on and could cause trouble, so again they met with pain and disappointment. Again, they reversed it and sought God's direction. The Mathews decided to open a rest house for the caravans who came by the compound regularly. They could provide medicine, shelter, and animal housing, and share the gospel with those who went into the villages to sell wool or buy barley, flour and other supplies. It was with great excitement that they worked to find a house, supplies and furniture. Many hours were spent getting it ready for opening day, which was to be December 8, 1950. However, on that very day, the Chinese troops decided to take it over and took up residence. There was nothing Wilda and Arthur could do.

The police arrived and announced that the Mathews would not be allowed to do any work in the village, period. No medicine, no tracts, no preaching and no meetings were permitted. All white people were to remain inside the compound. This was the fifth great disappointment they had faced. They had been treated poorly upon their arrival, denied the bare necessities of comfortable living quarters, shut out of helping to evangelize the Chinese church, and now forbidden to open their Mongol Gospel Inn. The last blow came as the police informed them they could no longer do anything outside the mission compound and were confined to their quarters.

Can you imagine their discouragement and the pain they were suffering? They could have been tempted to give up, be angry, get bitter at the Chinese, and even at God, for bringing them there. In their human strength, there were times of doubt. But, because of their desire to be obedient to their precious Lord, they would go to their little prayer corner in the kitchen and ask God to help them *not fear when heat comes* and *not be anxious in a year of drought nor cease to yield fruit (Jer. 17:8b)* . Comforted by their Lord, they rose from their knees to see what could be done for the Lord in spite of the situation they faced. In the compound were three Chinese missionary boys who needed training, support, love, and encouragement. The doors were still open to them, so Wilda and Arthur turned their efforts towards helping these young men. By doing this they were not cursing, nursing, rehearsing, or dispersing the hurt. They were reversing it by helping anyone they could and continuing to be faithful despite the setbacks they encountered.

The day finally came when the Mathews prayerfully sought God's direction for the future. He led them to apply for exit permits to leave China, as it was getting very dangerous to stay there. All China Inland Missionaries had been told to leave the country as soon as possible. Arthur writes:

> *We have tried everything with all our hearts, and had faith that the Lord would have something for us here, but He has shown us clearly that the doors are shutting **purposefully at His willing,** so with clear consciences we can think about trying the only door that seems open at the moment.*

Every item to be taken out of the country had to be registered with the government, so they tried to sell as much as they could to make departure easier. The cheery little curtains in the kitchen and the tablecloth that made their abode a little homier were sold or given away. Their dishes and household items were given to a Christian Russian family who had come into town. The Mathews were down to just tin plates and mugs which would be used for their journey home, and a pressure cooker. They expected to be gone within the week. Exit permits were filed on January 3, 1951, and their hopes were high as they kept receiving word of other missionaries getting their permits to go home.

As they waited for those all-important papers to arrive, they were met with continual delays and harassment by the Chinese officials. Days and weeks went by with glimpses of hope, only to be met with closed doors and harsh treatment by the officials. It would be two long years of near starvation, little or no heat, near-death illnesses for little Lilah and Wilda, rising and falling hopes with each official contact, and being forsaken by friends on the compound. Why would God allow this to happen to His servants? Why did they have to wait two more long, lonely years before returning home? Of course, we don't know all the reasons why God allows His beloved to go through such pain; but, I do know how much my life has been touched by their faithfulness.

While I was in a particularly difficult time, a dear friend handed me a little book entitled, **Green Leaf in Drought,** which is now out of print. I devoured it. I was occasionally tempted to think, *If only You had not moved us here, we wouldn't be without a job now.* Now I was reading how this dear missionary was tempted to doubt with her, "if only we had not come to this place." Listen to Wilda Matthew's heart in the midst of the pain. While alone in her bare kitchen, she suddenly remembered two tracts. One was *Second Causes* by Hudson Taylor and the other was A. B. Simpson's *The IF in Your Life* where she read the following portion:

> *I do not discount the "if" in your life. No matter what it is . . . come to the Lord with your "if" and let Him say to you what He said to Martha. He met her "if" with His "if"! Said I not unto thee that if thou wouldst believe, thou shouldest see the glory of God? The glory of God is to come out of the "if" in your life. Do not be thinking of your "if". Make a power out of your "if" for God. . . . Do you know that a light is to fall on your "if" some day? Then take in the possibilities and say, "Nothing has ever gone from me, that I shall not be better for God by it. . . ." Face the "if" in your life and say, for this I have Jesus.*

Because of their testimony, I wrote out on a note card, *If you believe, you will see the glory of God.* I kept this on my kitchen counter for six months and claimed it every day. Then I practiced saying, "for this I have Jesus!" when doubts arose or when fear or loneliness set in. I would repeat it over and over until it became a continual thought process that lifted me to new heights of peace.

In the second tract, Wilda read, "The secret of Hudson Taylor's rest of heart amid such tempests of hate was his re-fusal to look at second causes. . . . He believed it was with God, and God alone, he had to do." When his dear wife died, Hudson Taylor wrote, "If satisfied with His will and way, there is rest." After reading this, Wilda wrote, "The heart conflict has been terrible, but peace and quiet reign in both our hearts now. We can only sit still, trusting all things to work together."

At the same time, Arthur wrote:

> "Thou didst it" *is the text that I have before me these days and so we refuse to question, or complain even though the days may seem to have no sense in them. Thine hand presses me sore; not another's, but Thy hand!*
>
> *These trials of faith are to give us patience, for patience can only be worked as faith goes into the Pressure Chamber. To pull out because the pressure is laid on, and to start fretting would be to lose all the good He has in this for us.*

During this painful waiting time, I learned, as Wilda and Arthur had, that I had some ungodly layers to peel off; the layer of looking to blame others, the layer of resentment, the layer of wanting financial security, and the layer of wanting answers in my time. If these saints could trust God with all the pain, discouragement, and loneliness they had suffered, I could certainly trust Him in my situation.

> *Blessed be the God and Father of our Lord Jesus Christ, the Father of mercies and God of all comfort; who comforts us in all our affliction so that we may be able to comfort those who are in any affliction with the comfort with which we ourselves are comforted by God. For just as the sufferings of Christ are ours in abundance, so also our comfort is abundant through Christ. (2 Cor. 1:3–5)*

As I read the rest of their story, I was continually amazed at their faithfulness despite bitter disappointments and even Arthur's imprisonment for false accusations against him. Finally, two and a half years after their application to leave, they were miraculously freed to go. Wilda and Lilah went first, and Arthur followed several months later. It was on July 23, 1953, that the news was received that all 601 adults and 284 children from the China Inland Mission had evacuated Communist China. Not one was martyred. The Mathews were the last ones to be freed, but their testimony and faithfulness has touched thousands of lives.

If the Mathews had stayed in the hurt, there would have been no victory, no growth, no peace, no help to those on the Mission compound, no testimony to impact my life and the lives of others, no lessons of faith learned. There would have been only regrets at the missed opportunities. Are you dwelling on the hurt and missing God's plan for you? There's so much we can learn only by going through the fire His perfect will allows. **By reversing the hurt we are putting His mercy on display for others to see.**

Just as I was writing this page, I stopped to get today's mail. In it was a letter from someone in the Northwest who had not only heard me speak at a retreat, but had watched us go through our year of drought in the Seattle area. She shared how our faithfulness had ministered to her and her family, and that they would never be the same because of what God did in and for us. Again, I thank God for his grace for He alone is worthy to be praised!

And God is able to make all grace abound to you, that always having all sufficiency in everything, you may have an abundance for every good deed (2 Cor. 9:8).

CHAPTER 7

I CAN DETERMINE TO HELP OTHERS WHILE WAITING

It's so easy and human to become in-grown and self-centered when we're waiting for God to answer our prayers or change our circumstances. From the time we wake until the time we fall into bed, we are consumed with our needs and frustrations. Without responding to the Holy Spirit's call, we forget there's a whole world out there that needs to know the Savior. It was through our morning devotions together that Jim and I became keenly aware of the importance of reaching out to others each day. We determined that, no matter what our situation, we would each look for someone to encourage or share the Lord with on a daily basis. Maybe it was a phone call or a note; sometimes it was someone we met on our daily walk. Other times God would bring someone to us who was struggling with bitterness and anger over an unjust situation or disappointment. It was amazing to me how God flooded us with opportunities to share His word and His promises once we opened our eyes and hearts to His plan.

I love to collect rocks along the San Diego beaches and then display them in an attractive bowl in my home. People are always amazed at the colors, shapes, and beauty of each rock and assume that I bought them. One day, my daughter and daughter-in-law were admiring them and said they wanted to collect some to display in their homes. I took them to my favorite beach and said, "Here they are!"

They looked around, then looked and me and said, "But they seem so plain and ordinary." "I know" I replied, "but when you look at them individually, you begin to notice all sorts of things." Their search began, and "oohs" and "aahs" and "look what I found" soon followed. After taking this all in, Monica, my eight-year-old granddaughter called to me and said, "Nana, I think this is how God sees us. We sort of all look the same, but each one is special to Him." It was so true! Sometimes we just see a sea of ordinary or even dull people, but a closer look reveals individual beauty, unique characteristics, and even pain-filled eyes.

For Thou didst form my inward parts; Thou didst weave me in my mother's womb. I will give thanks to Thee, for I am fearfully and wonderfully made; wonderful are Thy works, and my soul knows it very well. My frame was not hidden from Thee, when I was made in secret, and skillfully wrought in the depths of the earth. Thine eyes have seen my unformed substance; and in Thy book they were all written, the days that were ordained for me, when as yet there was not one of them. (Ps. 139:13–16)

In our desire to help and encourage others, it's important to look for their special qualities, not their imperfections, and build them up accordingly. Let me explain. While speaking at a weekend retreat, I noticed that certain little goodies or snacks would often appear on the rear table of our meeting room. These weren't the planned refreshments prepared by the retreat committee. They were thoughtful additions like chocolate-covered spoons in a decorative basket near the coffee and beautifully arranged special candies and nuts. The strange thing was that no one ever saw anyone putting them out or replenishing them. They just seemed to appear out of nowhere for our enjoyment. I have to admit, if I were to do something like that, I'd probably make sure I was seen putting out the homemade goodies so that someone would comment on how wonderful they were. (Not a great motive for servanthood, I admit.)

The second day of the retreat, I asked the retreat chairperson if she knew who was responsible for this thoughtful idea. She pointed out a shy, plain-looking lady and said, "She really doesn't want to be noticed." I could tell at a glance that this lady probably suffered from low self-esteem, so I asked God to help me encourage her in some way and let her know how special she truly was. After the evening message, I found her and told her how much I appreciated her special touches, complimenting her on the attractive presentation and thoughtful planning. I asked her when she did it all. "Oh," she responded with moist eyes, "I come in after everyone's in bed or while they're still eating and just put a few things out. It's just something small I can do. I can't speak like you do."

I knew right then that God had brought me to this retreat for two reasons: one was to encourage and love this beautiful servant of the Lord, and the other was to learn the importance of humility in our service for the Lord. I couldn't help wondering if her service was more pleasing to God than mine that day. While seeking to minister to someone else's needs, God was reminding me of a true servant's heart.

A Servant's Heart

Do I have a servant's heart
or do I seek attention
for things I do in ministry
that someone might not mention?

Do I seek to help someone
who's heart is filled with pain?
Or am I only moved to act
by something I might gain?

Do I let the Holy Spirit
guide my deeds and thoughts each day?
Or do I contemplate a need
then go my selfish way?

Do I see with Jesus' eyes
those near me in despair?
Do I understand God's purpose
is for me to show **His** care?

Do I have a servant's heart
as I go about today?
Will I truly please my Savior?
As He leads, will I obey?

—*Carol Hopson*

Do nothing from selfishness or empty conceit, but with humility of mind let each of you regard one another as more important than himself; do not merely look out for your own personal interests, but also for the interests of others. (Phil. 2:4–5)

I could share many examples of God's faithfulness in bringing hurting people into our lives, but one story seems to stand alone. I had received a call from my beloved father that the doctors had found cancer in his bladder. Following surgery, he was going to need chemotherapy. In his eighty-four years of life, he had never been hospitalized. My dad had always been healthy and strong, so this news was shocking and hard to hear. As his first chemo treatment drew near, I desperately wanted to be there to offer support, so I flew down from Seattle to help him and my mother go through this difficult time. It's seldom convenient to help others, and that was the case in my life. I definitely wanted to go and be there with them, but the circumstances were difficult. I had to cancel several speaking engagements and Bible studies and change lots of plans in order to go. Also, Central California, where they lived, was having rare thunder storms and flooding everywhere. I only share this to point out that other's needs don't usually fall into our time schedule. We must trust God to work out the details of changed plans. On the flight down from Seattle, I asked the Lord to use me any way He chose and to really open my eyes for someone who might need God's love. I knew I needed to be there for my mom and dad, who had served the Lord so faithfully all their lives and whom I dearly loved, but I wondered if there was someone else God was bringing me down to help.

My dad was scheduled to have the treatments three days in a row, for three to four hours each day. This would be repeated at three-week intervals. I would drive him and my mother through the rare torrential storms to the chemo ward, help him get settled, and then would sit on a stool by his feet and hold his hand, making sure he was comfortable and warm while the treatment entered his body. This was the third day of the treatment and dad had fallen asleep, so I took my mom to a doctor's appointment and then planned to return to pick up my dad. We had about an hour before he would be finished, so my mother asked if I'd like to stop for coffee or some other treat. Knowing me, she thought I would probably jump at the opportunity, but something inside me said I needed to get back to the chemo ward right away, so we hurried back.

Upon our arrival, I checked my dad and found him awake, but doing fine. I wondered why I felt the rush to return. There were seven other patients receiving chemo treatments in recliner-type chairs. The chairs were arranged in a semi-circle in a comfortable, living room-type setting, with the nurse's desk at the center of it all. As I sat on my stool, I looked to my left and noticed a young man I hadn't seen when we left. I asked him how he was doing and he responded, "Not very well."

In the next few minutes I learned that he had melanoma, which had gone undetected at his last checkup. The doctors had given him six to eight weeks to live. He told me about his two young children and his wife and that he didn't know what to do. He was so miserable and had no answers for them about what was going to happen to him.

I looked down and saw a Bible he had checked out of the library tucked into the cushion of the chair. I said, "Well, you certainly brought the right book with you."

He replied, "It hasn't done me any good. I've been reading it, but I have no peace."

"Would you like to know how to have peace?" I asked.

"You mean you can tell me that?" he asked, looking at me with searching eyes.

I told him about two or three times in my life when I had faced the fear of cancer and other fearful situations, and how God's word had given me peace because of my relationship with the author. Then the Holy Spirit led me to turn to Philippians 4:6,7.

Be anxious for nothing but in everything by prayer and supplication, with thanksgiving, let your requests be made known unto God, and the peace of God which passes all understanding shall guard your heart and mind in Christ Jesus.

"Could you read that again? he asked.

By this time, every eye in the room was on us: the nurse, the other patients, the visitors in the waiting area, and my mom and dad. It seemed as if no one moved or breathed for the next fifteen minutes.

"I'd be happy to," I quickly answered. In a loud, slow voice, I re-read the same passage. "Would you like to know how to have the kind of peace that passes all understanding and guards your mind?"

"I'd give anything to have it," he replied, as his voice gave away the fear he was experiencing.

At this point, the Holy Spirit helped me clearly go from scripture to scripture, showing him what Jesus Christ had done for him. I showed him how the gift of salvation, forgiveness of sins, and eternal life in heaven was awaiting him if he chose to give his remaining days to the Lord.

"I can help you do it right now if you want to," I eagerly voiced.

"Yes, I want to. Would you please help me?" he responded.

I glanced at my dad, who had tear-filled eyes. I knew he was praying for us. I took the young man's hand in mine, with the IV drip still flowing into it, and had him repeat each phrase of the prayer after me. Not a soul stirred in that ward that day. The nurse never moved from her station to change anything. Before this, she was always buzzing around, checking the patients and changing the bags, but not now. It was as if the Lord had stopped everything so that nothing would distract this precious soul from entering the Kingdom.

When we both finished praying, I looked up at his face and asked, "Bruce, how do you feel?"

He replied, "I have peace!" He said it with such confidence and with the first smile I had seen on his face. "I really have peace!" he said again.

How good of God to allow each of those patients to hear the whole gospel and the prayer of confession and faith. Each one was facing an unknown future, and only God knows how many of them turned to Him because of Bruce's testimony of peace.

After that, the Lord gave us about 15 more minutes before my dad's treatment was finished. Together, Bruce and I read scriptures of the assurance of salvation and his secure future. I wrote down verses he could read to help when doubts and fears reappeared, and verses to help him face the future unafraid.

As I was helping my dad get ready to leave, Bruce's wife walked into the room to meet him. He shouted, "This is Carol. She brought God to the chemo ward today!"

How I praise God for the great privilege of being His hands and His voice in that fear-filled place. When we ask God to open our eyes to others and use us for His glory, He does. There is no greater joy! Helping others while waiting changes our focus, reminds us of our priorities, and gives us something about which to rejoice.

CHAPTER 8

LEARN TO ACCEPT THIS SEASON OF LIFE

While living in the Pacific Northwest after fifty years in California, I certainly had to learn to accept the seasons. In Solvang, I was accustomed to weather that varied between sunshine and an occasional cloudy day, so the seasons were definitely new to me. I asked the Lord to help me enjoy the days without sun, the cold temperatures, and yes, even all the rain. The Lord seemed to teach me much about life by accepting the seasons I now lived in.

A New Season Brings New Sights and Insights

As I let go of the sunny, blue skies I was accustomed to, I opened my eyes to the beautiful new sights around me.

67

Since we arrived in the fall, I was overwhelmed by the colors of the changing leaves, the luscious green of the grass, and sight of streams and lakes everywhere. As the fall settled into winter, Seattle had the heaviest snowstorm in over thirty years. I had the new sights of snow-covered yards, trees, and driveways! The gorgeous Olympic mountain range could be viewed from my kitchen window, and though it was usually covered with clouds, it was a spectacular sight when the clouds lifted.

All of this was very different and very cold, but the Lord put it on my heart to accept it, enjoy what I saw, and even delight in it. For a California girl this was truly a miracle from the Lord. As I faced my new waiting situation, with no idea of what God was going to do with us, I realized that I could ask Him to help me enjoy the new sights of this season of my life.

In the day of prosperity be happy, but in the day of adversity consider God has made the one as well as the other so that man may not discover anything that will be after him. (Eccles. 7:14)

Since God made these days for me also, I could learn to enjoy the outward sights as well as the new insights he brought into my life. One very gray day several months into our unemployment, the Lord began to reveal some things to me that I didn't like admitting. I had become secure in our home and our material surroundings in such a short time. It brought such joy, and I saw it as a gift from the Lord since I didn't have my family around. But I had begun to cling to the gift, rather than the Giver, so God had me do some housework. As I walked from room to room in my beautiful home, I observed that it was really only "wood, hay and stubble" in God's eyes, and it needed to be thrown on the altar. With my hands stretched out and facing upward, I walked from room to room and said, "Lord, I give this gorgeous kitchen back to You. Heavenly Father, I give You back this beautiful view of Puget Sound. Thank you for loaning it to me for these short years. I release the downstairs bedrooms and playroom that my grandchildren love to You." Each room in the house was given back to the great Giver of everything. When I finished, there was an overwhelming sense of peace in my heart. *I delight to do Thy will O God; Thy Law is within my heart (Ps. 40:8).*

Has God given you some new insights in your waiting season? Are you listening and have you acted on them, or are you still hanging on to what you wish this season would bring? When we put our hopes and our joy in material things or circumstances, we rise and fall emotionally with new seasons. But when we put our hope in the Lord our Rock, we enjoy emotional stability. David knew this truth too well:

I love Thee, O Lord, my strength; the Lord is my rock and my fortress and my deliverer, My God, my rock, in whom I take refuge; my shield and the horn of my salvation, my stronghold. (Ps. 18:1–2)

Do you see any material possessions, people, or circumstances that David is clinging to? No, he has learned to cling to Someone who is permanent, unchangeable, and totally secure. Let me share with you the importance of clinging to the Lord our Rock when in a difficult season.

The Rock gives Permanence

We can never count on life going on the same, year after year. We can't rely on financial security, friends, family, or our health; but we can definitely find security in our relationship with our Lord and the truths of His precious Word. These truths give us a permanent foundation for raising our children, for the marriage relationship, for self-evaluation, for daily direction, and for our purpose for living. Our core values don't change with the times or with the circumstances.

My Rock

The Lord is my Rock.
Be still my soul and learn
To cling!

The Lord is my Rock.
Don't fear or look about
Just sing!

The Lord is my Rock
What can I find to fear?
Nothing!

—*Carol Hopson*

The Rock gives Perspective

Have you known someone who sees the world through rose-colored glasses? They always see the good, the beautiful, the best in others. Unfortunately, I'm not like that. I definitely need the Lord to help me see with His eyes; otherwise, my perspective can easily be tainted by my own self-centered viewpoint.

During our thirty-four years of marriage, my husband has often asked me to join him in a variety of athletic exercises such as tennis, golf, biking, hiking, etc. Since sports were not a big part of my upbringing, my outlook has always been quite different from his. He sees the fun of being together, the exhilaration of physical exercise, the challenge of doing your best.

On the other hand, I see being uncomfortable, getting sweaty, not being able to do it well, and an aching body. We approach the activity with two completely different perspectives, so our responses and expectations vary greatly.

This is the problem when we are faced with new seasons in our lives. We look at it through our upbringing, our fears, our emotional state, and our dreams. Our perspective isn't clear. God's word reminds us:

> Now the God of peace, who brought up from the dead the great Shepherd of the sheep through the blood of the eternal covenant, even Jesus our Lord, equip you in every good thing to do His will, working in us that which is pleasing in His sight, through Jesus Christ, to whom be the glory forever and ever. Amen. (Heb. 13:20–21)

Did you notice that very important phrase about perspective? *Now the God of peace . . . equip you in every good thing to do His will.* To do His will, we need His perspective, not ours. The promise is that God will equip us to do His will in each season and situation of our lives, if we align our perspective with His. How do we do this? The passage goes on to say, He is *working in us that which is pleasing in His sight.* Let me share three ways we gain His perspective because of our relationship to the Rock.

First of all, we need to **believe** that the battle has already been won.

> What shall we say then? Are we to continue in sin that grace might increase? May it never be! How shall we who died to sin still live in it? Or do you not know that all of us who have been baptized into Christ Jesus have been baptized into His death? Therefore we have been buried with Him through baptism into death, in order that as Christ was raised from the dead through the glory of the Father, so we too might walk in newness of

71

life. For if we have become united with Him in the likeness of His death, certainly we shall be also in the likeness of His resurrection, knowing this, that our old self was crucified with Him, that our body of sin might be done away with, that we should no longer be slaves to sin; for he who has died is freed from sin. (Rom. 6:1–7)

D. Martyn Lloyd-Jones writes, "This is, to me, one of the most comforting and assuring and glorious aspects of our faith. We are never called to crucify our old man. Why? Because it has already happened . . . the old man was crucified with Christ on the cross." We have the wrong perspective so often. We think we can't help our sinful nature, our sinful thinking that leads to doubt and discouragement and eventually defeat. But, that is Satan's work of deluding us into thinking we are still *in Adam*, rather than *in Christ*.

Secondly, we need to **study** the mind of Christ by reading and meditating on His word. Our Lord's mindset is clearly expressed in Paul's epistle to the Philippians.

Have this attitude in you which was also in Christ Jesus, who, although He existed in the form of God, did not regard equality with God a thing to be grasped, but emptied Himself, taking the form of a bond-servant, and being made in the likeness of men, and being found in appearance as a man, He humbled Himself by becoming obedient to the point of death, even death on a cross. (Phil. 2:5–8)

After reading about our Lord's willingness to give up His rights, empty Himself, and humbly obey His Father to the point of death on the cross, we begin to understand the perspective we need to have. Again, Satan would deceive us into thinking this is too difficult, too painful, or even impossible. That's why it's so important to remember that the battle has already been won in Christ's death on the cross. Now, it's simply a matter of choice. In Psalm 51:12, David pleads, *Restore to me the joy of Thy salvation and grant me a willing spirit to sustain me* (NIV). What is it that sustains us? It is a willing spirit for whatever God brings into, or takes out of, our lives. Remember that it is the Lord who equips us to be willing. We just need to ask.

When our children were young, there were times when they disobeyed us and we needed to discipline them according to God's word. In the "discipling" and disciplining process, Jim or I would always ask, "What did you choose to do?" Initially, there were all kinds of creative reasons given for the disobedience. "He pushed me first," or "I didn't remember what you said," and so on. But as we continued the process, we always narrowed it down to a choice. "What was the right thing to do, and did you do it?" Eventually, they learned that there were no excuses for disobedience except their own selfish choice, which always brought consequences. This is what we need to realize in our Christian walk. We need to stop making excuses for our wrong choices, and choose obedience. It was so interesting for my husband and me to notice that, at any given time, the level of peace and happiness in our children was directly related to whether they were making right choices or not. As soon as they could speak, we began praying with and for them that God would help them make good choices which honored him.

When my son's daughter was almost two, I observed an incredible scene in our home. Monica had wandered into our bedroom and was admiring the Precious Moments® figurine on my dresser. Her parents had taught her what to touch and what not to touch—so she knew this was just something to look at—but it was so inviting and so eye-level. As I stood behind the door, I watched her little hand reach out to pick it up and quickly draw back. She stared at it, thought for a minute, and then reached again, never quite touching it. She repeated this process four times. After jerking her hand away the last time, she turned away, started walking, and said, "Good girl!" I'll never forget the joy I felt as I observed that tender little heart deciding to make the right choice. That must be the way our Heavenly Father feels when we make a difficult decision to obey and praise Him.

Third, we must **pray** for a Godly perspective on our situation. As Easter of 1999 drew near and we still didn't have direction from the Lord, we continued to pray that God would help us see things through His eyes, and not through human eyes. He kept imprinting our hearts with faithfulness and praise. Rather than dwelling on the future, we were to be faithful to the God who plans and knows our future. Rather than wasting our energy on worry, we were called to praise. While reading one night, I came upon a phrase that caught my eye. It was, "In the center of the circle of the will of God, I stand!" As God often does, He awakened me early Easter morning with this praise:

In the Center of the Circle

In the center of the circle
of the will of God I stand!
I cannot see my future now,
but trust it to His hand.

This morning I will praise Him
as I face this bright new day.
And think of all He's given me
and from doubts turn away.

I do not know what lies ahead
my future is unknown.
But God has promised each of us
He dearly loves His own.

74

And He will show me just in time
His purpose and His plan,
As in the center of the circle
of His will I stand.

—*Carol Hopson*
Easter 1999

When I was obedient to God's word and asked Him to help me believe it, practice it, and share it, there was always sustaining peace and joy because I no longer had my perspective in view, but His.

CHAPTER 9

A New Season Requires a New Wardrobe

When winter came to Seattle, it definitely required a change in clothing. My old wardrobe consisted of sandals, sun dresses, and sweaters that were just right for California living. But the need was very different in the Pacific Northwest. Now I needed warm socks, heavy sweaters, and coats—which I had never even owned, but were extremely necessary for this season in my life. Both types of clothing are important for their seasons, but wearing the right clothing at the right time is essential.

Though all the clothes that Colossians chapter three mentions are important, there are certain ones that seem essential for the waiting season. Colossians 3:12 says:

> And so, as those who have been chosen of God, holy and beloved, put on a heart of compassion, kindness, humility, gentleness and patience; bearing with one another and forgiving each other, whoever has a complaint against anyone, just as the Lord forgave you, so also should you. And beyond all these things put on love, which is the perfect bond of unity. And let the peace of Christ rule in your hearts, to which indeed you were called in one body; and be thankful.

The meaning of the phrase "put on" here, is *to be clothed with.*

Clothed with Humility

The clothing of humility is usually essential while waiting because nothing is going as we planned and the circumstances often are a blow to our pride. When my husband was out of work for twelve months, it was definitely a humbling time; but in searching the Scriptures, I found how precious humility is to our Lord. I Peter 5:6 tells us, *Humble yourselves therefore, under the mighty hand of God, that He may exalt you at the proper time, casting all your anxiety upon Him, because He cares for you.*

Matthew Henry puts it this way, "Let your minds, behavior, garb, and whole frame be adorned with humility, as the most beautiful habit you can wear; this will render obedience and duty easy and pleasant." I understood this to mean that I needed to totally accept the place and circumstances I was in, as they were appointed by God. No matter how I had been treated or mistreated, my obedience to the Lord and His Word would show if I was willing to wear the clothing of humility that pleased my Lord so much. *Humble yourselves in the presence of the Lord and He will exalt you* (James 4:10). We also read that God gives His special grace to those who are humble. *But He gives a greater grace. Therefore, it says, God is opposed to the proud, but gives grace to the humble* (James 4:6).

What would the clothing of humility look like?

1. I would be aware of my own shortcomings and not so quick to judge others (Phil. 2:3–4).
2. I wouldn't dwell on my hurt feelings, but on God's healing power (Eph. 4:31–32).
3. I wouldn't worry about what people think, but only what God thinks of me (Col. 1:10).
4. I would allow God to work in me, and for me, however He chooses (Rom. 8:28).
5. I wouldn't get angry with unjust situations, but would leave the results with Him (1 Pet. 2:21–23).

Why are we so opposed to humbling situations? I think it's because we have become so self-absorbed and self-centered. We think that if we follow Him, God owes us a wonderful life, free from humiliating situations. How wrong that thinking is! If it weren't for all the painful, growing, pruning, humbling times in my life, I would never know that special "greater grace" of my Savior. I would not know the incredible joy and fruitfulness that comes from faithfulness and steadfastness in the midst of the storm.

Why don't you try thinking of your humility wardrobe as a blessing? Since God loves the humble, it must be very special to Him. That should be enough for us.

Clothed with Patience

Sometimes while waiting, we get tired of wearing our clothing of patience. I know there were times when I wanted to exchange it for anything else in my spiritual wardrobe. Sometimes it's so difficult to put on and continually wear because it means we are to bear our trials sweetly, without grumbling.

> Do all things without grumbling or disputing; that you may prove yourselves to be blameless and innocent, children of God above reproach in the midst of a crooked and perverse generation, among whom you appear as lights in the world, holding fast the word of life, so that in the day of Christ I may have cause to glory because I did not run in vain nor toil in vain. (Phil 2:14–16)

As I read these verses, I see four important reasons for waiting patiently:

1. By not complaining about my situation, I am living in obedience to the Lord.
2. As others watch me, I will truly be a light to those around me.
3. I will be able to rejoice at the Lord's coming, because I remained faithful during the tough times.
4. The painful waiting times are not in vain. God will use me as He sees fit if I am obedient to His word.

As I observe my grandchildren, I see that patience is one of the most difficult lessons for them to learn. Sometimes there are tears, sometimes there is a battle for a certain toy, and often those precious little faces show total frustration at not getting their way. But their loving, godly parents are always there to discipline them when necessary and teach them to share, to give up their wills, and learn to obey. Recently, my daughter and I were enjoying lunch at a courtyard cafe while her two little boys, ages two and four, played around a central fountain. They suddenly decided they both wanted the same Matchbox® car, and, as you would expect, it quickly grew into a frustrating situation for all. Jennifer stepped in and took the boys aside, disciplined them, and calmly and lovingly reminded them of their need to share with each other and take turns. I watched from our table as two-year-old Jack said, "I sorry Eyeat!" Elliot (four years old) responded with, "I forgive you Jack!" This was followed by a big hug between the two.

I had seen this many times before—as this was the normal training process in their home—but it certainly wasn't normal for those at the outdoor cafe who were watching. Though we were unaware of the impact, one lady later came up to my daughter and said, "I couldn't believe what I saw. My boys would never do that. I don't know how you got them to do it." She went on, "Just wait until they're older; they won't do it then." My daughter and I know differently. The reason we know is because Hebrews 12:11 promises, *All discipline for the moment seems not to be joyful, but sorrowful; yet to those who have been trained by it, afterwards it yields the peaceful fruit of righteousness.* You see, the proper training, repeated over and over, yields the peaceful fruit of righteous living. I saw this in my own children's lives, in my older granddaughters' lives, and now the word of God was working in my grandsons' lives.

Discipline

Oh how difficult it is
to see your precious child
decide to disobey you
and do it with a smile!

Because you love this little one
you care enough to take

the time, the strength, the rod of love
an obedient child to make.

How difficult for God to see
his precious little child
decide to do things his own way
mile after mile.

Because He loves His little lamb
He tenderly does take
the time to discipline in love
a Godly soul to make.

—*Carol Hopson*

You might wonder what this has to do with patience. When we lack patience, we are stepping out of God's will and choosing our own way. Sometimes it hurts others, and it always hurts us because our fellowship is broken. Our loving heavenly Father may need to use some form of discipline to bring us back to the peaceful fruit of righteousness.

The good news about patience is found in Colossians 1:11. We are *strengthened with all power, according to His glorious might, for the attaining of all steadfastness and patience.* God is the One who strengthens us with His power to enable us to be steadfast and patient. How wonderful! I don't have to muster it up on my own; just read His word, believe it and obey it, and He'll do the rest.

What would the clothing of patience look like?

1. Patience doesn't react in bitterness or anger (Eph. 4:29, Col. 1:12–13).
2. Patience gives others grace to fail again and again (1 Cor. 13, Eph. 4:32).

3. Patience waits on God alone for answers and fulfillment (Ps. 27:14; 37:3–7).
4. Patience responds with love and obedience when the emotions want to do otherwise (Col. 4:6, Eph. 4:1–2).
5. Patience believes God's lovingkindness will prevail (Ps. 136:1–26; 147:11).

Sometimes, like Jack and Elliot, we need to say, "I'm sorry, Lord," for discarding my patience clothing. He's waiting to say, "I forgive you" and give us a great big hug. The more we practice this, the easier it becomes. We're renewed and revived again by His strength and love.

The Overcoat of Peace

And beyond all these things put on love, which is the perfect bond of unity. And let the peace of Christ rule in your hearts, to which indeed you were called in one body; and be thankful (Col. 3:14,15). When we read that the peace of Christ is to "rule" in our hearts, it means to let peace be the umpire, the deciding factor in all situations. Where there is conflict in motives, desires, or our will, let the peace of Christ win. What rules in our hearts will be evident in our lives. If our waiting has made us angry, fearful, resentful, or worried, then that is what others will see in us. Therefore, the overcoat of peace is crucial for the believer who wants to shine for the Lord.

Everywhere I went—whether at church, at a retreat or seminar, or with friends—someone would ask, "Has Jim found a job yet?" I had to make a choice each time, to either wallow in self pity, or let the peace of God be what they saw first in my life. My answer would usually be, "No, he hasn't, but God is faithful and His grace is sufficient!" Just being faithful in that small way seemed to bring on more of His amazing peace and provided an opportunity to share more with others. It would lead to questions about how to trust in difficult times, or what verses meant the most to me, etc. It was amazing to me how this question brought opportunity after opportunity to magnify the Lord—if I was consciously wearing my overcoat of peace.

One mother, after sitting through three messages at a retreat, approached me tearfully and asked, "How can I have what you have? Your husband is out of work, you've been unfairly treated, and you don't even know where you're going, but you have such peace. My husband makes a great salary, and we have a beautiful 5,000 square foot home, but none of it brings peace." What a privilege to show her where peace was found and to pray with her as she accepted God's wondrous gift of salvation. I never expected this to happen, and it wasn't to my credit. It was God's grace alone that was sufficient to keep me peaceful and trusting. He's waiting to do the same thing in you.

Last year, my husband took our two granddaughters for a walk through a wooded area behind their home. After walking a little while and climbing over a few fallen trees, Becca, the youngest, got tired and looked up at her Papa and said, "Papa, I can't do it. Please help me." Now what do you think her Papa said to her? "No, Becca, do it yourself!" Or "I'm too busy to help you"? Of course not! He was delighted that she wanted to be carried and needed him. (He was always looking for excuses to hug them anyway.) I think this is how our heavenly Father feels when we turn to Him and say, "I need you to give me your peace; I can't do it anymore." He responds with, *Peace I leave with you; My peace I give to you; not as the world gives, do I give to you. Let not your heart be troubled, nor let it be fearful* (John 14:27).

What would the overcoat of peace look like?

1. Peace would be the first thing others would see in my countenance (John 14:27).

2. I would remain content even when the waiting dragged on (Phil. 4:6–7).
3. I would spend time daily in the Word and in prayer to make sure my trust was totally in the Lord (Ps. 119:165).

Have you updated your wardrobe for this waiting season? It might make you a lot more comfortable in your situation.

Seasons

I woke one day and found that I
was in a brand new season.
It took me by surprise and so
I didn't like the reason.

It wasn't what was comfortable
and not what I would choose.
I didn't want my life to change
I had so much to lose.

This season brought uncertainty
on almost every side.
I couldn't cling to things on earth
or in my friends confide.

Humility and patience were
the clothes I needed now
to get me through this trying time
but God would teach me how.

To wear them daily for my Lord
and thank Him for His word

And trust that God's sufficiency
from my mouth would be heard.

For as I chose humility
pride had to step aside
And Satan had no power then
so had to run and hide.

And how could he cause me to fret
if patience was my choice
He couldn't have a victory
'cause praise rang through my voice.

And then the overcoat of peace
protected from the cold.
and kept my heart both soft and warm
and easier to mold.

So in this season of my life
I trust my Father still.
For nothing comes to me without
first passing through His will.

—*Carol Hopson*

Practicing Praise Is Essential While Waiting

Several years ago, while remodeling our home in Solvang, California, we decided to put in a beautiful, ceramic tile floor. I had taken care to pick out something I really liked and was so eager to see it all laid in our newly remodeled kitchen. We eagerly awaited the finished work and admired it greatly. It had turned out beautifully; the color was so rich and unusual. I especially enjoyed it. However, after about three weeks, I started noticing hairline cracks throughout the floor. I was heartsick! When my husband saw it, he called the man who installed it. He said he'd be over soon to replace it, which he did. We all decided it must have been faulty tile. But, to my great dismay, it happened again in about three weeks. I couldn't believe my eyes—my beautiful floor was cracking again. We called the tile man, who came and replaced the tile again. Each time the peach-colored tile had to be jackhammered out, it left a fine dust all over the house and in every cupboard and drawer. It was a mess that required hours of vacuuming and mopping to get everything clean again. After replacing it two times and after it started cracking the third time, we were told that the problem was in the foundation. No matter how many times they replaced it, it would continue to crack because the foundation was not poured correctly.

As I asked the Lord why this was happening, He gave me a wonderful illustration that I have used many times in my life and have shared often with others. No matter how great we try to look on the outside, or how "together" we try to appear on Sundays or in front of others, the cracks will appear if our foundation isn't settled and sure. When our boat was rocked by my husband's sudden loss of work, it was the foundation of our lives that the Lord had lain that kept us afloat. Part of that foundation was built on the practice of praising the Lord at all times. *I will bless the Lord at all times; His praise shall continually be in my mouth (Ps. 34:1).* I had seen my godly parents practice this; they in turn, taught it to me as I was growing up.

When my children were young, I was constantly reminding them to say, *please, thank you,* and *no, thank you.* The teaching seemed endless, and I wondered if they would ever remember without being reminded. Then one glorious, memorable day, they began to say *please* and *thank you* all on their own. It had been practiced for so long that it had become a habit. What a wonderful habit! Better still, it never left them.

Just as manners don't come naturally, praise is not a natural response to waiting. But with God's help, it can become natural if we are willing to practice it. God's word does not give us an "out" for not praising Him during the tough times. On the contrary, we are urged time and again that praise should be our first thought. Listen to God's instructions and then check yourself to see if you've been practicing praise.

I will give thanks to the Lord according to His righteousness, and will sing praise to the name of the Lord Most High. (Ps. 7:17)

But let all who take refuge in Thee be glad, let them ever sing for joy; and mayest Thou shelter them, that those who love Thy name may exult in Thee. (Ps. 5:11)

Sing for joy in the Lord, O you righteous ones; praise is becoming to the upright. Give thanks to the Lord with the lyre, sing praises to Him with a harp of ten strings, sing to Him a new song; play skillfully with a shout of joy, for the word of the Lord is upright and all His work is done in faithfulness. (Ps. 33:1–4)

And He put a new song in my mouth, a song of praise to our God; many will see and fear, and will trust in the Lord. (Ps. 40:3)

He who offers a sacrifice of thanksgiving honors Me; and to him who orders his way aright I shall show the salvation of God. (Ps. 50:23)

Willingly I will sacrifice to Thee; I will give thanks to Thy name, O Lord, for it is good. (Ps. 54:6)

When I am afraid, I will put my trust in Thee. In God, whose word I praise, in God I have put my trust; I shall not be afraid. What can mere man do to me? (Ps. 56:3–4)

But as for me, I shall sing of Thy strength; yes, I shall joyfully sing of Thy lovingkindness in the morning, for Thou hast been my stronghold, and a refuge in the day of my distress. O my strength, I will sing praises to Thee; for God is my stronghold, the God who shows me lovingkindness. (Ps. 59:16–17)

But as for me, I will hope continually, and will praise Thee yet more and more. My mouth shall tell of Thy righteousness, and of Thy salvation all day long; for I do not know the sum of them. (Ps. 71:14–15)

I could go on and on about David's heart of praise seen in the Psalms, but I think you've gotten the picture. Do you see how David kept practicing praise? If you read the preceding or following verses in each of these passages, you can see that David's circumstances were not what he would choose. He was being pursued by enemies, fearing attacks, in emotional pits, hiding from Saul, persecuted and weary from old age, and yet, he practiced praise continually. Notice that he praised God for who He was, for His strength, for His word, for what He did in him, for being in control of everything, for His faithfulness in the past, and for the privilege of honoring Him through praise. **This praise wasn't based on his circumstances, but on His knowledge of and trust in his God. Since the object of his praise never changed, he could praise in any and all situations.**

On a recent mission trip to Korea, we were exposed to a new level of praise. While singing in a home for forgotten elderly people, we were touched by a dear lady in her eighties. She just wanted to praise God for everything, though it seemed that she had nothing—no family, no real home, very poor surroundings, seemingly forgotten by the world and friends. Yet, to see and hear her sing, "Jesus loves me this I know" in Korean—as tears of love streamed down her face—

brought conviction to my heart as well as the student's hearts who had come to minister there.

How could she be so filled with praise? I believe she knew what mattered to God and had probably practiced praising Him for many years. It was now a perfectly natural response, based on her love for her Lord and not on her surroundings (or lack of them). It was a lesson we used with the students continually. We reminded them that praise shouldn't be a response only in good times, but any time, if our foundation is correct and we care about what matters to God.

What Matters to God?

Have you ever stopped to think for awhile
what meeting the Lord will be like?
What will you think of when His face you see?
It could even happen tonight!

Will you tell Him about the degrees you acquired
through hard work and many long years?
Will you boast of your home and the things that you own
that bring you such stress and such fear?

Maybe you'll tell Him you wore the right clothes
from Nordstrom, with labels to show
that you bought the best that money could buy
and wanted your neighbors to know.

Or maybe you'll try to explain to the Lord
how busy you were with your plans;
and how doing His work just didn't quite fit,
so back to your comfort you ran.

These things will not matter when His face you see.
It's what has been done in His name.
Will there be stars in your crown of life?
Or will choices you made bring you shame?

What matters to Him is a heart that is set
on doing His will above all,
by loving, forgiving and *praising His name*
and always obeying His call.

It has to begin with a choice that you make
to please Him and not yourself.
For all you've collected materially
will someday be left on a shelf!

—*Carol Hopson*

I shall never forget the most vivid, life-changing example of practicing praise I have ever heard. When I was young, my parents, Dr. and Mrs. Ralph Kraft, often visited the missions in foreign countries that our church supported. Their purpose was to encourage the missionaries, preach in the newly established churches, and teach classes wherever needed. On their first trip to India, they visited a leprosy hospital where they were taken to a meager, upper room where the worst leprosy cases were. Let me share it in my dad's own words.

Almost forty years ago, my wife, Dorothy, and I made our first trip to India. One of the most outstanding things we saw was the leprosy hospital. A friend of ours was in charge, and one of the nurses came from our church in the states. She said, "Pastor and Dorothy, would you like to visit our five princes?" "Who are they" I asked. "They are five lepers, all of whom are absolutely blind. None of them have fingers on their hands, nor toes on their feet. They are confined to a room on the second floor where they each have a straw mat for a bed." She told us that all five of them had become devout believers in Christ as Savior and Lord. She also invited us to meet with them and talk to them about Scripture and pray with them. This we did gladly. When we saw them, we were moved beyond words by their sad condition, and their continual, joyful praise to their God. Every time we went back to India for the next thirty years, we wanted to visit the five lepers because they were such dear, trusting Christians. They never saw daylight, they could not feed themselves, nor could they walk, yet the nurses told us that they never, ever heard any complaints from them.

Just a few years ago, on our last trip to India, we went back to the leprosy hospital. I asked, "Are the five princes still here?" I found out that all but one had gone on to Glory. One remained who was very sick and eager to go to heaven, too. We again went up to visit him, lying on his straw mat in the dark upper room. There was that dear saint who loved the Lord so much. The nurse said, "Pastor, speak to him, and we'll see if he remembers you." When he heard my voice, he put up his feeble arms and—with his stubs—tried to clap. The nurse leaned over to hear what he said, and then she repeated it to us. "He wants you to know that he remembers you and has prayed for you, every day, for over thirty years." My wife and I went out in the hall and cried.

When we left India, I said to the Lord, "I am your servant, but I need to know how, not why, but how those lepers lived over thirty years on a straw mat, in their helpless condition without complaint. They sang hymns day or night and never complained about their situation. I need to know how that is possible." When I came home, I began to search the scriptures as to how God's people suffered so terribly. Beginning back in the book of Genesis, I came very quickly to the words, "Noah found grace in the eyes of the Lord." I thought to myself, perhaps this is a clue, and it was. As I moved through Scripture, I read that Esther found grace, and that Daniel found grace. Throughout Scripture, that phrase popped out as the answer, namely, that God gave them all grace. My question now is, what is that grace?

In researching the meaning of grace, I found that it is not only the unmerited favor of God. It has to do with **God giving special power to His children so they can do what they would not otherwise be able to do.** Because of this they can praise God in the midst of terrible conditions. Ephesians 2:8–9 tells us that grace is a gift from God. James 4:6 says, "He giveth a greater grace." I came to the conclusion that since God made those five lepers content and happy for over 30 years in their condition, he could and would do that for me. He could certainly meet our needs and keep us victorious in any and all circumstances of life, by His grace.

What my dad learned through that experience and the ensuing study of grace changed his ministry forever. Thousands were strengthened, encouraged, and challenged because of it.

Those five men never knew how their praise was used by God; often it's the same way with us. We just need to be faithful to praise Him in our circumstances and allow God to use us in ways we could never imagine or even know about. God's grace—so beyond our understanding!

God would never ask us to praise Him continually without giving us the grace to do just that.

CHAPTER 11

CLAIM THE UPHOLDING POWER OF GOD

Do not fear for I am with you;
Do not anxiously look about
you, for I am your God.
I will strengthen you, surely I
will help you,
*Surely I will **uphold** you with*
my righteous right hand.
—Isaiah 41:10 (emphasis added)

When fear invades our lives, due to a circumstance that is unexpected or out of our control, the choices we make determine our peace, or lack of it. Each new day brings an opportunity to claim the power of God or the opportunity to sink into despair.

The Lord tells us, *Do not fear*; therefore, it's important to know what fear is. Fear is really unbelief parading in disguise. It's not trusting the Creator of the universe to handle our problem. Fear and faith can never exist together. Either fear will drive away our faith, or faith will drive away our fear. When I was fearful about our future—where we would live, how we would survive without a salary, and so on—I was disobedient to my Lord because I was actually doubting his upholding power. Fear then paralyzes us and keeps us from thinking right thoughts and doing the right things.

In order to activate our faith and claim God's power we need to change our focus:

1. From Problems to Possibilities: (**All God has in mind for our growth and maturity.**)

For I am confident of this very thing, that He who began a good work in you will perfect it until the day of Christ Jesus (Phil. 1:6.) Have we automatically ruled out that there could be great possibilities in our lives because of this situation? Just because we can't see them doesn't limit the God of the universe. Now that my husband and I are in a wonderful new ministry we love, and we see our family and grandchildren more than we ever dreamed of, it's easy to see the possibilities God had in store. But oh, how I longed to see them on those dark days in Seattle! It would have been so much easier to trust. I knew that I was in God's refining fire, sometimes willingly and sometimes not so willingly. But through the fire came an intense relationship with my Savior that nothing else could shape. Isaiah 48:10 says, *Behold, I have refined you, but not as silver, I have tested you in the furnace of affliction.* According to the dictionary, to be refined means "to reduce to a pure state, to purify." During the purifying process of waiting, the Lord taught me to re-focus on eternity and let go of the world around me.

One Day Closer to Glory

One day closer to glory
that's why my heart can sing!
For things on this earth are not lasting,
never to them should I cling.

Houses are only a framework,
where love and contentment abide;
and wealth won't be needed in heaven
where some day real soon we'll reside.

So let's keep our focus on heaven
and all that eternity brings . . .
Together with all the beloved
and great hymns of praise we will sing.

No sickness, no heartache, no moving,
and never saying good-bye.
Oh what a day of rejoicing
when Jesus appears in the sky!

We're one day closer to Glory.
Today other thoughts shall flee.
Tomorrow our Savior may take us
to live with Him eternally.

—*Carol Hopson*
April 6, 1999

When we can agree to the refining process and focus on what's really important and what God has in mind for our growth, then we can willingly accept the refiner's fire and take hold of the upholding power of God.

2. From Problems to Priorities: **(Learning to think with a renewed mind.)**

No soldier in active service entangles himself in the affairs of everyday life, that he may please the one who enlisted him (2 Tim. 2:4.) My priority always is to please the One who enlisted me, Jesus Christ. To get tangled up in the worry and fear of a situation that I cannot change takes me out of active service. No wonder I feel discouraged and defeated when I don't stick to God's priorities for my life.

3. From Problems to Promises: **(Claiming the power through applying God's Word.)**

Blessed is the man who trusts in the Lord and whose trust is the Lord. For he will be like a tree planted by the water, that extends its roots by a stream and will not fear when the heat comes; but its leaves will be green. And it will not be anxious in a year of drought nor cease to yield fruit (Jer. 17:7–8) Here, we are promised that if we trust the Lord in difficult times, we will never need to be worried or afraid because we will continue to be healthy and fruitful. And Isaiah 41:13 reminds us, *For I am the Lord your God, who upholds your right hand, Who says to you, "Do not fear, I will help you."* How many times I have held the hand of one of my children or grandchildren to keep them from falling. Sometimes they would slip and begin to fall, but my hand was there to support and uphold them, and keep them from harm. If they chose to pull away from me, they would usually get hurt. But if they let me help them, there were no tears. It's when we pull away from our Heavenly Father's hand by our fear, that we slip. He didn't let go; we did.

4. From Problems to Perspective: **(Trying to see things from God's perspective.)**

Seeing that His divine power has granted to us everything pertaining to life and godliness, through the true knowledge of Him who called us by His own glory and excellence. For by these He has granted to us His precious and magnificent promises, in order that by them you might become partakers of the divine nature, having escaped the corruption that is in the world by lust (I Pet. 1:3–4). A biblical perspective on waiting brings us to victory because we believe that God has given us *everything pertaining to life and godliness.* We can face any situation through claiming His *precious and magnificent promises.* Though we can't see His plan, we can claim His promises.

Since we began this chapter with the biblical admonition, *Do not fear,* it is now important to note what kinds of things make us fearful. The fear of:

- losing a loved one,
- losing our pride or place of respect,
- losing the security of a job and finances,
- loneliness,
- another person's influence or power over us,
- known or unknown circumstances we can't control,
- being asked to do something beyond what we think we can handle.

All of these are real and can cause deep pain, but this portion of God's word commands, *Do not fear for I am with you.* Then how does God's presence with us calm our fears in these situations? In Psalm 118:6 we read, *The Lord is for me, I will not fear what man can do.* Man is not in control of what happens to me, God is! Even in a case where you have been treated unfairly, you don't need to focus on the person, but on the power of God. He is still in control, and you can thank Him for that and allow Him to work it all out as He sees fit. Psalm 138:8 tells us that *The Lord will accomplish what concerns me.* None of the above causes of fear can keep the Lord from accomplishing what concerns me. The only things that will interrupt His plan are my unwillingness to trust and my choice to go against His word in making a decision.

One of my favorite verses with which to fight fear is found in 1 Peter 4:19. *Therefore, let those also who suffer according to the will of God entrust their souls to a faithful Creator in doing what is right.* If I have put Him first in my life and am trying to live a life that is pleasing to Him, the important thing here is knowing that God has allowed my suffering. As I live in obedience to Him, I can trust that whatever He allows— loneliness, heartache, unknown future, unfair treatment—I can trust my *faithful Creator* to do what is right. What a relief that has been for me.

At twenty-four years of age, I was pregnant with our second child. Jim and I had desperately wanted another child after our son, Jeff, was born, and we felt this was exactly the right time to enlarge our family. We had prayed that God would bless us with the children He desired for us, and we were tremendously excited about the birth of another precious child. When I was almost four months pregnant, we decided to take a plane trip to Portland, Oregon, to see some college friends of ours. While in flight, I had a serious complication and began hemorrhaging. My heart was sick, because this baby was already so precious to me and I knew this meant trouble. When we landed, I immediately received medical care and was told that I would either miscarry soon, or that something was definitely wrong with the baby. We would find out shortly whether there was a heartbeat or not. The only other possibility was that my baby would have serious mental or physical problems, or both. The doctor felt certain that these were the only options, but in my heart, I knew that God would do whatever He chose, despite the doctor's predictions. I began to pray for God's peace and upholding power to get me through the next six months.

When we heard the heartbeat for the first time, there was great rejoicing. As the baby grew in my womb, there was more praise. That very special grace, mentioned in the previous chapter, was so real in my life. I seldom talked about the problem to anyone; I just left it in my Great Physician's hands. If I needed special grace to handle the loss of this child or the birth of a special-need's child, I knew He would give it to me. His grace was absolutely sufficient to keep me peaceful and even greatly anticipating this child's birth— even though the human outlook was very grim.

On March 9th, 1970, a beautiful, healthy, perfect baby daughter entered our lives. You could have heard me shout, "Thank you, Lord!" all over the hospital. My husband's eyes were filled with tears of thanksgiving. God chose to give us this precious, healthy child and we have been forever grateful. In my heart, I also knew that He would have seen me through anything else He chose for me because His upholding power during those six long months had no limits.

Upholding Grace

The grace of God is so beyond
all human thoughts of mine.

It reaches to the depths of me
and will not be confined.

This grace has met me in despair
and brought me through my pain.
It's helped me wait through trials long
and trust in Jesus' name.

Believing in God's promises
and claiming them in prayer,
This wondrous, all-sufficient grace
has met my every care.

So thank you God for your great plan
your mercy and your grace,
For with the comfort of your love
this waiting I can face.

And trust you with my deepest fears
and things that hurt me so.
Please help me now to faithful be,
so through this I will grow.

—*Carol Hopson*

CHAPTER 12

THE REST OF
THE STORY

Throughout these chapters, I have shared many personal experiences of waiting and trusting God, most of which came about because of God's change of plans for us last year. After reading my first book, "But God, This Wasn't My Plan", many of you asked that I write the rest of my story to tell what God did on our behalf. This chapter is dedicated to the Lord in gratitude for His plan, purpose, and abundant grace in our lives.

About six months into our waiting without employment or direction, my husband was invited to a large Christian School in southern California for a preliminary interview to become the school's Headmaster. In early

February, we made the trip to sunny San Diego, about fifteen miles south of the school. As we were met at the airport and taken to the school, we prayed that God would show us His plan by giving us peace, or a special sign that this was the place He had for us. We had been on other campuses and received other invitations, but we never had peace that they were the places for us, so we waited.

As we drove onto the campus, Jim and I were immediately struck by the school's sign. It had an eagle on it, with this verse inscribed below. *Yet those who wait for the Lord will gain new strength, they will mount up with wings like eagles. They will run and not get tired, they will walk and not become weary (Is. 40:31).* I had taught this verse so many times; it had become very special to me. I had studied the eagle for many years and learned that he is very different from most other creatures. This is especially true in a storm, as I mentioned in the chapter on loneliness, but let me explain further. Though the eagle has binocular vision and can see the storm approaching from a great distance, he does not seek cover like other wildlife. Instead, he remains on some high perch or on the edge of his nest and awaits the oncoming storm. As he sees others run in fear, he remains unafraid and calm. As the high winds begin to blow and shake the trees and even his nest, he stays still and waits. It's not until the first few drops of rain begin that he launches into flight (*mounts up*) and locks his wings into an ascending position. He then uses the strong currents of the storm to help him circle round and round, gaining more height with each lift. Eventually, through his calm perseverance and knowledge, he is lifted above the storm into the warmth of the sunlight above. The storm still rages, but he has risen above it and is not affected by it.

I've so often taught this as the way the Christian should respond to the storms or waiting periods of life. We should be continually studying and memorizing God's word so that we are able to withstand and rise above any storm that confronts us. *Thy Word I have treasured in my heart that I may not sin against Thee* (Ps. 119:11). *Thou hast ordained Thy precepts, that we should keep them diligently* (v. 4). The eagle's preparation is very important, because he never knows when the storms will appear. It is the same with us.

When I saw the eagle in flight on the school's entrance sign, my heart began to pound and I felt the presence of the Lord. While my husband was meeting with the Search Committee members, a dear board member—one of the "school fathers"—took me to a lovely place for tea. He told me the history of the school and how it was really a "miracle school" that God had blessed each step of the way. I heard story after story of godly people trusting God for every crisis they faced, and then the impossible coming about through God's grace.

It sounded so much like our story in Solvang, California, that I could hardly believe my ears. Over the past thirty-four years, we've listened to many people tell stories of how a school got its building or finances. But we've seldom heard people give all the praise to God, realizing, as we did, that it was totally a day-by-day miracle that the school survived. We felt so strongly, and shared freely, that the Christian Academy we had begun in Solvang had survived and thrived because God did wondrous, miraculous things on our behalf and for His glory. Now I was hearing this same passion, excitement, and commitment from this board member. My heart was definitely being tugged and touched by God.

After Jim finished his meetings that day, we sat in the motel room and prayed and shared our thoughts of the day. Excited but hesitant, we both shared that our hearts were moved by the people we had met and their passion and love for the Lord and the Christian School ministry. It was almost too good to believe that such a place was looking for a Head-master. However, we also knew that they had done a nation-wide search; there were over one hundred applicants for the position. We didn't know God's plan for us, but there was definitely a desire to pursue this opportunity further.

As we left the sunshine and flew home to the rain and the unknown, we continued to wait on the Lord. Now that we had a seen a place where we could serve and where we felt God might lead us, you might think that the waiting became easier. On the contrary; it became more difficult. As the days turned into weeks and then months—with still no answer about our future—we needed to take another example from the eagle.

The eagle knows the importance of being prepared each day for what lies ahead. Each morning he will spend at least an hour preening his feathers. During this process, the eagle passes each feather through his beak, where he cleans and waterproofs it using his preening gland. This preening prepa-ration is extremely important for facing a storm or capturing prey in the water. It both cleans and protects the feathers. **Every morning, Jim and I needed to "preen" for the day ahead by cleansing our minds of doubt and filling them with God's promises for protection.** Sometimes, the discour-agement was almost overwhelming. Yet if we had spent time in God's word and prayer together, we were prepared to face Satan's fiery darts and claim the promise or provision we had read that morning. It would always help us rise above the problem and see the "Son," instead.

We made three more trips to that wonderful school, each about a month apart. The Search Committee was made up of godly people who wanted to know God's will; they were doing a very thorough, difficult job. Each time we attended more meetings, answered more questions, and fell more in love with the people and the school. And each time we went home not knowing what their choice would be. We knew there were several other wonderful Christian men that they were seriously considering; only God knew what their decision would be.

Waiting's for the Birds!

Okay Lord, I've had enough
this waiting's for the birds!
I'm tired, discouraged, and out of sorts;
my prayers You haven't heard!

Can't You give me just one hint
of what Your will might be?
Won't you send me some small word
so I can trust in Thee?

You say I have just what I need
if I will only see
That You are with me every day
to give me victory.

You say I don't need answers now?
That faith should be my aim?
'Cause trusting you and keeping sweet
brings glory to Your name?

Oh yes, I think I've got it Lord!
With You I'll be content.
And worship You and claim Your peace
unworried 'bout the rent.

> I cannot change my circumstance
> but I can change my mind
> And focus on just pleasing You
> and then contentment find.

> —*Carol Hopson*

During these long months of waiting to hear, the Lord opened numerous doors to share His love and grace with others. Before each retreat at which I was asked to speak, the organizers—without knowing my circumstances—gave me titles like, "Step up to Faith," or "A Heart of Obedience," or "Trusting through Trials," or "Faith that Moves your Mountains." Do you see a pattern here? As I shared where we were in the waiting process and how completely sufficient my Lord was, God worked in hearts beyond my greatest expectations. I couldn't have shared this if it wasn't true, and each time God miraculously met my needs and gave me joy as I spoke again and again of His sustaining grace. He knew there were struggling hearts that needed to hear that message while I was still waiting for His plan. I can thank Him for His purpose in making me wait so others could come to know Him.

At the beginning of May, after the rainiest winter in Seattle's history, eleven long months of waiting without work (except for odd jobs my husband could pick up to put food on the table), and when it seemed all opportunities for employment had passed, we were called to come back to the school we had fallen in love with. My husband was offered the position of Headmaster, and it was with great joy that he accepted. Then God's plan began to unfold. In the introduction of this book, I told you that the first buyers who walked into our home bought it, and they did. However, after a few weeks, they backed out of the purchase. We now had a house to sell quickly, as we needed to move in just one month. The market was very slow in the Pacific Northwest due to the heavy rain. The average time for selling a house was five months, so we needed a miracle. After being offered the job, Jim and I were rejoicing and praying in the motel room when the phone rang. Our Realtor said, "The previous buyers are back with a full price offer, and this time they're sure!" Hallelujah, what a great God!

The next morning, we began looking at homes in the San Diego area that would meet our specific needs. We were flying home the following day and asked the Lord to help us find a home quickly. We didn't want to get sidetracked looking; we wanted to move on to more important things like getting acquainted, settling into the new job, and ministering to people. We needed a one-story home with a large spare bedroom, because my parents would be spending a lot of time with us in the winter. We also asked God for enough bedrooms for the family visits and a yard the grandchildren could enjoy. God so abundantly blessed us! Out of the thirty homes we looked at, only one had any kind of yard; it was the only one-story house we saw. Most of the homes are two stories in order to conserve space and build more houses on the valuable southern California coast. Finding a one-level home with a very large spare bedroom, a den close by for my parent's comfort, and a beautiful, spacious yard with a built-in play yard for the grandchildren was a special gift from God.

Beyond all this, the Lord moved us to within a two-hour drive of our daughter's family and four hours from our son's family. We now have frequent visits from our parents, kids, and grandchildren, which is more than we ever dreamed we'd have again. He gave us back the sunny warm climate I had learned to be content without, and he gave us incredible new ministries we loved right from the start, because we knew beyond a doubt that this was the place He had planned for us all along. New friendships, new challenges, new goals, new insights, new opportunities to touch lives, and new ways to praise Him are all a part of His gift to us.

Now that I've been here for over six months, I'm still amazed at how . . . *God causes all things to work together for good to those who love God, to those who are called according to His purpose (Rom. 8:28).* The lessons I have learned have been far-reaching; I lovingly urge you to take a different look at your waiting period.

1. Change your attitude!

If you're still struggling with waiting for a person or situation to change, let me encourage you to *cease striving* and know that He is God (Ps. 46:10a). In other words, *change your thinking!* Why waste your time and energy on worry and frustration? Who does that help and what does it accomplish? God's word says, *Little children, let us not love with word or with tongue, but in deed and truth (1 John 3:18).* What we believe is evidenced by our actions. Are you acting as if there's no hope, or as if you have a God who loves you and knows what's best for you?

Maybe you need to get to know your Heavenly Father all over again. Remember, *You know that it was not with perishable things such as silver or gold that you were redeemed from the empty way of life handed down to you from your forefathers, but with the precious blood of Christ, a lamb without blemish or defect (1 Pet. 1:18 NIV).* If your Heavenly Father loved you enough to give His Son so you might have eternal life, don't you think you can trust Him with your pain? In *The Message,* Eugene Peterson paraphrases 1 Peter 4:1–2 as follows: *Since Jesus went through everything you're going through and more, learn to think like Him. Think of your sufferings as a weaning from the old sinful habit of always expecting to get your own way. Then you'll be able to live out your days free to pursue what God wants instead of being tyrannized by what you want.*

2. Practice praising God.

Through Him then, let us continually offer up a sacrifice of praise to God, that is the fruit of lips that give thanks to His name (Heb. 13:15). Do you love Him enough to sacrifice your loved one or situation on the altar of thankfulness to Him? It was only when I was obedient to the Lord in this area that I found peace in the storm. God's word is so clear on this, yet we often make excuses for our grumbling spirit. There are no excuses in God's eyes, only obedience that brings glory to Him and peace to us.

To offer this *sacrifice of praise to God,* we must accept what He has provided for us so far. Let me explain. On one of our granddaughters' first visits to us in southern California, we decided to take them to the newly opened Legoland®. After enjoying a great day of fun, we took them to the gift store to buy a souvenir before we left. Four-year-old Becca chose a small Lego® flashlight, rather like a penlight, and as soon as we arrived home she wanted to try it out. "Nana, can you help me find a dark place?" I showed her the large closet in our bedroom and she eagerly went in with her new purchase, closing the door behind her. Shortly, she opened the door, ran out, and called her seven-year-old sister Monica saying, "Moni, come in here with me! It's dark, but don't be scared. I have a 'lashlight'!" You have to realize what a small light this tiny penlight shown in our large closet, but it was enough to remove her fears.

It made me realize I'm often not content with the "lashlight" God gives me, because I want a floodlight! I want to see the whole picture and everything surrounding it; then

I will be thankful. God doesn't promise a floodlight, but He does promise to light our path just enough for today. *Thy Word is a lamp to my feet, and a light to my path (Ps. 119:105).* Will you sacrificially thank Him for the light He has given through His precious Word, and then focus on obeying the light you have?

3. Look for opportunities to bear fruit.

So that you may walk in a manner worthy of the Lord, to please Him in all respects, bearing fruit in every good work and increasing in the knowledge of God (Col. 1:10). The joy of bearing fruit during a difficult time is so rewarding that I want you to experience it. Once you see what God wants to do in and through you, you won't want to live any other way. Start your day not looking at what troubles you, but by asking God to use you in miraculous ways. Then keep your eyes and heart open to follow His leading. While finishing a last-minute trip to pick up a Christmas gift, I stopped at a restaurant where there was a waiting line out the door. I saw a vacant seat at the counter, so I proceeded there. As I sat down, I asked God if there was someone on either side of me who needed to hear about the real reason for Christmas. If so, He should please let me know. I began a conversation with one woman who was finishing her meal. She left shortly afterwards, so the woman on my right became my focal point. As I asked questions, she began sharing how materialistic her children had become; they had everything and still weren't satisfied. She ended by saying, "Christmas just drives me nuts!"

Okay Lord, I guess this is the one who needs to hear about You. As the Holy Spirit gave me the words, I proceeded to share why Christmas was so special to me and what made it that way. Her heart was ready and open. She stayed and listened, and even shed some tears as she heard the message of

God's love. It wasn't difficult; it was just a matter of asking God to help me bear fruit for His glory. He did just that.

4. Ask God to create a clean heart in you.

Many times I've had to confess that there is nothing good in me and that I have failed again, especially in the area of my thoughts. Some days I would be bombarded with discouraging thoughts that would lead to a root of bitterness or resentment. I would need to pray this verse, *Create in me a clean heart, O God, and renew a steadfast spirit within me (Ps. 51:10).* As we seek God's forgiveness and then ask Him to create, or make from nothing, a clean heart within us, we must give up our agenda and be totally open to what He wants to do. This means letting go of the "what if," "if only," "how come" and "this isn't fair" thoughts, and replacing them with "whatever you want, Lord!" and "for this I have Jesus!" thoughts. Then, Satan is defeated and we are renewed and enabled to be steadfast in serving Him.

5. Desire to be single-minded!

Again, let me tell you a story about my grandchildren. When one of my granddaughters was about twenty months old, I bought a Barney® book because she loved that children's TV personality, and I knew she would be excited. When her next visit came, I called her to my lap and began to read her the story about Barney on the farm. She looked at the first page and adoringly said, "Barney," with great emphasis on the word. Each page pictured Barney feeding one of the animals. As I turned the pages, I asked her what the cow says, and she responded, "Baaaaarney!" putting her little finger on Barney's face. I tried again on the rooster page and asked if she would tell me what the rooster says, knowing she knew the barnyard sounds very well. But, the only answer I got for each page was,

"Baaaaaarney!" as she adoringly kept her eyes fixed on the object of her affection. When I got to the final page and again tried my tactic of, "What does the cute little piggy say?" she took my face in her tiny hands and pulled it directly facing her. "Nana," she said, "it's Baaaaaarney!"

It was a great lesson for me on being single-minded. Nothing sidetracked her from seeing Barney because that was all she was interested in. What sidetracks you from seeing Jesus? Paul says, *But what things were gain to me, those I have counted as loss for the sake of Christ. More than that, I count all things to be loss in view of the surpassing value of knowing Christ Jesus my Lord, for whom I have suffered the loss of all things, and count them but rubbish in order that I may gain Christ* (Phil. 3:7–8). To be single-minded while waiting, is to say with Paul that the value of knowing Christ Jesus my Lord is so much more precious than having my own way. Therefore, I am content in my situation and only concerned about gaining more of Christ's character and knowledge through the experience. When faced with waiting, the true object of my affection and commitment will be obvious.

How precious and miraculous to know that God chooses to use us in the midst of our waiting, when we choose **single-minded obedience.**

In this I greatly rejoice:
- that stumbling blocks can be turned into stepping stones,
- that the act of praise defeats Satan,
- that God has upheld me through every storm,
- that learning humility is precious to God,
- that He gives a greater grace when needed,
- that His plan is better than my plan,
- that waiting has brought me incredible growth and blessing,

- that God chooses to use me even though I feel unworthy,
- that the power of God is greater than the plans of men,
- that God still abundantly blesses those who choose to trust Him.

As you've read the rest of my story, you may think that I no longer need to wait on the Lord for anything. Everything sounds so perfect, but let me assure you that life is not like that. Though I greatly rejoice in God's answers to my prayers, there are still things for which I am waiting —such as relief from a painful, continual physical problem from which God has not chosen to free me. But this keeps my focus on trusting Him each day for my specific needs in this area, and it gives me the opportunity to praise Him in spite of the pain. It helps me have more concern for others who live with pain and encourages me to pray for them. It reminds me that God could heal me at any time, but until He does, He will help me continue to be fruitful and faithful. It also gives me moment-by-moment opportunities to be obedient in my attitude. Yes, there's always something for which we will wait, but the learning and growing on the road of life is worth it all.

The Road of Life
Author Unknown

At first, I saw God as my observer, my judge, keeping track of the things I did wrong, so as to know whether I merited heaven or hell when I die. He was out there, sort of like a president. I recognized His picture when I saw it, but I really didn't know Him.

BUT GOD, I'M TIRED OF WAITING!

But later on when I met Christ, it seemed as though life were rather like a bike ride; it was a tandem bike, and I noticed that Christ was in the back helping me pedal.

I don't know just when it was that He suggested we change places, but life has not been the same since. When I had control, I knew the way. It was rather boring, but predictable. It was the shortest distance between two points.

But when He took the lead, He knew delightful long cuts, up mountains, and through rocky places at breakneck speeds; it was all I could do to hang on! Even though it looked like madness, He said, "Pedal!"

I worried and was anxious and asked, "Where are you taking me?" He laughed and didn't answer, and I started to learn to trust. I forgot my boring life and entered into the adventure. And when I'd say, "I'm scared," He'd lean back and touch my hand.

He took me to people with gifts that I needed, gifts of healing, acceptance, and joy. They gave me their gifts to take on my journey, my Lord's and mine. And we were off again. He said, "Give the gifts away; they're extra baggage, too much weight." So I did, to the people we met, and I found that in giving, I received, and still our burden was light.

I did not trust Him, at first, in control of my life. I thought He'd wreck it; but He knows bike secrets, knows how to make it bend to take sharp corners, jump to clear high rocks, fly to shorten scary passages.

And I am learning to shut up and pedal in the strangest places, and I'm beginning to enjoy the view and the cool breeze on my face with my delightful constant companion, Christ. And when I'm sure I just can't do anymore, He just smiles and says, "Pedal."

116

Keep pedaling my dear friend! There's abundant grace just around the corner of obedience and joy beyond measure at the end of your journey.

In this you greatly rejoice, even though now for a little while, if necessary, you have been distressed by various trials, that the proof of your faith, being more precious than gold which is perishable, even though tested by fire, may be found to result in praise and glory and honor at the revelation of Jesus Christ (1 Pet. 1:6–7).

EPILOGUE

A Wee Small Child

A wee small child once asked the Lord
to come into her heart.
        She knew He did 'cause she
        felt glad
        and loved Him from the start.

And as she grew she knew that God
was with her every day.
        She sang to him and prayed to
        Him
        and didn't want to stray.

In second grade she tried to teach
a Bible class at school.
        But found out that was not
        allowed,
        for sure, she broke the rule.

She taught again at sixth grade lunch
with five of her good friends.
> But once again she was found out
> and that came to an end.

So life went on and she asked God
why she had such desire,
> to teach God's word and help her friends
> but others squelched the fire.

She waited through her schooling years
then on to Bible college.
> She studied hard and loved each day
> for she was gaining knowledge.

Then into her life came a man
of Godly character.
> And after years of courtship sweet
> he asked to marry her.

And on their wedding day they vowed
to serve their Lord as one,
> so when they met Him, He would say,
> "My faithful ones, well done!"

Up one hill and down another,
through the valleys low,
> the woman learned anew to trust
> for only God could know.

That all the joys and trials of life
were there for her to learn.
> So she could teach of God's great grace,
> as she so long had yearned.

And as she went through each hardship
another window came.
> She learned that what she'd just been through
> could bring God joy or shame.

Times of waiting, times of pain
not what she expected,
> But in His plan, 'twas no mistake
> but by His hand directed.

Her children grew and honored God
a joy beyond all measure.
> And God kept her in loving care
> a fact that she would treasure.

So she asked God to use her life
whatever it would bring.
> And she would speak and praise His name
> and to Him always cling.

How faithful and compassionate
her loving Father's hand.
> For using her to teach His word
> was part of His great plan.

And now her heart abounds with praise;
something I think you'll see.
> For that wee child who trusted God,
> by now, you know was me.

—*Carol Hopson*

To God be the Glory!

Index of Poems

Carol Hopson welcomes your inquiries regarding speaking engagements.

She can be contacted at

1015 Olive Crest Dr
Encinitas, CA 92024

E-mail address: logonjah@aol.com

To order additional copies of

BUT *God...*

I'm
Tired
of
Waiting!

Have your credit card ready and call

(877) 421-READ (7323)

or send $9.95 each plus $3.95* S&H to

WinePress Publishing
PO Box 428
Enumclaw, WA 98022

* add $1.00 S&H for each additional book ordered